Paolo Granat

Introduction to
Media Ecology

Paolo Granata
Introduction to Media Ecology

ISBN 979-8-7664-6988-9

© Paolo Granata 2021
First Italian edition: *Ecologia dei Media,* FrancoAngeli, 2015

All rights reserved. No part of this book may be reproduced or transmitted in any form or by any means, electronic or mechanical, including photocopying, recording, or by an information storage and retrieval system—except by a reviewer who may quote brief passages in a review to be printed in a magazine or newspaper—without permission in writing from the publisher.

*To my students.
Just like this book,
life is a work in progress.*

CONTENTS

Prologue 7

1. What is Media Ecology? 11

2. The New York School 23
    2.1 Lewis Mumford and the ecology of technics ... 25
    2.2 Susan Langer and the ecology of forms 34
    2.3 Neil Postman and media education 44

3. The Toronto School 55
    3.1 Harold Innis and the ecology of knowledge ... 58
    3.2 Marshall McLuhan and the aesthetics of media ... 68
    3.3 Walter Ong and the ecology of the word 84

4. Pioneering schools and thinkers 95
    4.1 The Chicago School and urban ecology 96
    4.2 Gregory Bateson and the ecology of the mind ... 111
    4.3 Edward Hall and cultural ecology 124

5. European roots 139
    5.1 The French scene 139
    5.2 The German tradition 146
    5.3 The British context 156

6. Media Ecology today 161

Bibliography 165

Prologue

There is a story that has been told for quite some time, reiterated a few years ago by the American literary legend David Foster Wallace. The story begins with two young fish swimming along easy and carefree. They happen to meet an older fish swimming the opposite way, who nods at them and says: «Morning, boys, how's the water?». The two young fish swim on for a bit, and then—eventually—one of them looks over at the other and wonders: «Water? What the hell is water?».

The moral of the story is quite apparent but far from banal. Sometimes we fail to realize what is most obvious. We take our surroundings for granted; but few people question if we are really aware of our surroundings. Many aspects of daily life are almost unknown to us precisely because they have always been part of our existence—our everyday experience—and therefore become almost imperceivable and invisible. Yet, the context that foregrounds human experience and becomes its foundation covertly impacts our development. The point is that we are not fully aware of our environment. The water, so to speak, is all around us and we have been swimming in it for a long time. Even Einstein questioned: «What does a fish know about the water in which he swims all his life?».

That question may well be the inspiration for the intellectual adventure described in this book. If water is the medium in which the two young fish swim in, what do we know about the media *in the midst of which* we lead our lives? This rhetorical question hides an insight. The media environment that surrounds us is in many ways imperceptible because we take it for granted—just like water was imperceptible to the two young fish. If we want to know more about this imperceptible presence, we need to start developing a new awareness of how we consider the media around us. This is not just a matter of getting to know or learn how to use these media. It means, instead, learning how to live with and within those media. Rather than considering media as mere tools, means, or channels that can be used more or less to our will, we should consider them for what they are—*actual environments*—within which we lead our lives; environments that shape our experiences.

Indeed, almost anything we think and feel happens within our contemporary media environment. Daily experience happens within these environments. Whether we want or accept it or not, whether we are aware of it or not, we act and live within the media; media really are our environment. That doesn't mean that our life is defined by the media, rather it constantly interacts with and is transformed by them in a process of mutual influence. In other words, the media are our habits and habitat, the infrastructure of that invisible and complex network that is the human ecosystem. Considering media in these terms means accepting the idea that there is an ecology of media that we inhabit and navigate daily.

During the 1960s, the Canadian thinker Marshall McLuhan—one of the pioneers of the intellectual tradition explored by this book—told his own story about fish and water that echoes Einstein's though is slightly more provocative: «Water is unknown to a fish until it discovers air». Well, it is that 'air' that is precisely what media ecology as a discipline is set to discover; a constant discovery we can never be sure of achieving once and for all that, in turn, becomes a sort of deliberate exploration of the deepest aspects of human culture.

This book offers an ecological approach to media studies, or an introduction to thinking about media as environments. I hope this approach may help whoever decides to read this book—students, scholars or general readers interested in the human condition of our time—start their own exploration with the awareness of being part of a larger human, cultural, social, and natural system; a forever open, dynamic, complex, and therefore endlessly fascinating and stimulating system. Media ecology is precisely aimed at promoting the kind of systemic perspective that underlies an ecological approach.

Living within the media with this kind of awareness means recognizing the role-playing game within which we are inevitably called to participate. Clearly, the rules of the game are made by us due to the constant process of social and cultural transformation that is inherent in human existence. And this book—as an attempt at presenting the authors, ideas and key principles of media ecology—is nothing but another step in the process of understanding those same rules. But, once the game is on, all we can do is play both *with* the media and *within* the media.

1. What is Media Ecology?

First of all, a definition

In 1968, the American scholar and later pop-intellectual Neil Postman (§ 2.3) chaired the annual meeting of the National Council of Teachers of English. There, he presented a paper that left a lasting mark on North American academia. Later published under the title *The Reformed English Curriculum* (Postman, 1970), the paper contained the first formulation of a new approach to media and communication research aimed at probing the complexity of human culture based on the interconnections of its manifold and articulated expressive forms. A broad array of theoretical and methodological principles led Postman to name this new research approach *media ecology*. The first pages of his paper offer a definition that effectively illustrates the peculiar features of an approach that was certainly original, if not downright unusual, for the time. Media ecology is defined as the study that «looks into the matter of how media of communication affect human perception, understanding, feeling and value» (p. 161).

To capture and consider the relationship of cultural and social environments with human life, the New York-based scholar used the term *ecology* in a broad and surprising way, drawing attention to the larger environment—the water—in which we inhabit. He further explains that an environment is «a complex message system which imposes on human beings certain ways of thinking, feeling, and behaving» (*id.*). Such a complex system—specifically, the network of mutual dependencies that influence human beings—is nothing other than the media environment. In *Teaching as a conserving activity* (1979), Postman is even more explicit in justifying the use of the term ecology to explain the observation of elements such as «the rate and scale and structure of change within an environment» (p. 17), without making distinctions between "man-made" and the more common "natural" environment that surrounds human beings. He viewed these two environments as one, as assemblages of nature and human invention, all the while emphasizing that it is necessary to carefully explore both. Within the definition proposed by the American thinker, the term ecology is indeed used according to its etymon—the Greek word *oikos*, meaning "household", "dwelling", "residence", combined with the suffix *logos*, "discourse"—therefore clarifying the relationship of ecology in its social, political, cultural meaning with the term "economy". Later in his career, at the opening of the Inaugural Convention of the Media Ecology Association (established in 1998), Postman explained once more why he had used the term ecology in that sense: «We put the word "media" in the front of the word "ecology" to suggest that we were not simply interested in media, but in the ways in which the interaction between media and human beings give a culture its character» (2000, p. 11).

Viewing media as environments, as the habitat where the changes that shape human culture are deeply rooted, implies a broader definition of the concept of "medium—a definition that embraces every aspect of human activity. According to the particular approach of media ecology, the media system includes so much more than the mass media as typically conceived: language, writing, print, radio, TV, the internet, to name just a few. Since every human artifact, invention, innovation, or insight should be considered *in media res*, "things in the middle"—based on the Latin expression this term comes from—or all around the human beings, they inevitably become part of the human environment. In other words, any medium helps establishing the habitat where human experience manifests itself. A medium is a cultural, technological, communication environment; an ensemble of the natural and the artificial—a context that shapes any human being's experience.

In Postman's words, media «are not mere instruments which make things easier for us. They are environments [...] within which we discover, fashion, and express our humanity in particular ways» (1979, p. 186). In other words, media ecology's peculiarly environmental emphasis effectively invalidates the common conviction that media are mere tools, instruments, channels, or devices that we use to communicate with each other or to interact with the world. The ecological approach implied by Postman's foundational description means that media can be defined as the entirety of the cultural, technological, and communication forms within which we live. It also means that media are not (or not just) instruments or tools. They are conceived as actual environments where human experience takes place and the complex and delicate process of human culture unfolds. Although quite nuanced, the definition of media as 'environments' was effectively a huge leap in terms of re-orientating media studies.

A systemic vision

Systems theoretical perspectives are the central, epistemological tenet of media ecology. Using an ecological approach to understanding media means approaching said media in terms of a systemic vision that conceives the interrelation of humanity and technology as a dynamic and open ecosystem that is unified and coherent, albeit complex. The media environment is a system of interconnected elements where the form and specific features of each media reconnect with the plurality of processes that take place in the larger environment, becoming networks of mutual relations and dependencies that lead each element of the system to interact with all the others. In the overall reality thus generated in this process, the individual elements coexist in a fundamental balance resulting from the constant and dynamic interaction of all of its components and are subjected to constant changes.

Adopting a systemic perspective enforces the environmental metaphor introduced by Postman and, consequently, the fundamental concept according to which media are environments. But such vision is also necessary to overcome the classic causal-deterministic folly and its failure to explain the processes and conditionings that influence human and social development. In its inflexibly linear interpretation, such approach implicitly viewed media as agents of change, independent subjects, and a decisive factor in technology or even in society. The systemic vision adopted by media ecology as an interpretive model can, instead, grasp the complexity of the media phenomena that equally and unlimitedly affect both the natural and the cultural sphere, both technological and the social factors, considered as closely complementary and mutually related fields.

Therefore, the ecological approach effectively and conclusively amends the principle of linear causality that cannot possibly penetrate the complex web of phenomena underlying human culture. By adopting an organicistic view of reality to study the interaction between human phenomena and their mutual systemic relationships, media ecology addresses the need to create a comprehensive and dynamic view of the entire variety of media forms, all while recognizing the central role of strictly communication forms. Only by considering all media as an environment, or an ecosystem, is it possible to conceive them as a habitat, a dynamic organism, within which the processes of change and transformation of human culture arise and in turn influence the system's very structure.

The systemic view also emphasizes recognition within the media environment of the dynamics, interaction, and exchange processes that constantly exist between the human beings and our technological and natural environment. Humanity is part of the environment we inhabit. Humanity and our technologies are one and the same system, and the relation of interdependence and reciprocity between the two is simply an expression of their coexistence, of the mutual influence they exert on each other. At the same time, media are an active and constant process that human beings are integrally part of; a complex process generated by the variety of expressive forms that have been developed and layered across human culture and history in a crossbreeding process that has gradually formed the very environments the human beings live in. In other words, the slow action that human beings have constantly exerted on the world is a process that in turn has influenced them. Human beings have always shaped their environments and have been shaped by it as the result of an interaction based on a, once more, organic, and systemic relation. In addition, the symbiotic relation between human beings and media environment is such that the former could not exist without the latter. The purpose of media ecology is the exploration of such relationships in all of its complexity, with a focus on the procedural and environmental dynamics that an ecological perspective—derived of systems theoretical thinking—may help clarify.

A field approach

Although Neil Postman undisputedly and formally introduced media ecology in American academia in 1968, his innovative ideas were actually the result of previous, foundational approaches to media studies stemming from early twentieth-century North American intellectual traditions. It is possible to describe a quite articulated scene of academicians who shared a peculiar and, in many ways, unusual interest in the interrelations of culture, technology, and communication. Such a focus was more than a mere disciplinary specialism and can rather be explained as a pursuit of different perspectives, although clustered within one field of inquiry. In fact, a rigorously interdisciplinary approach is one of the distinctive features of media ecology as a field of study. This book is an attempt to unify the contributions provided by a varied group of thinkers who effectively reshaped and revitalized the traditional fields of knowledge by recognizing original connections between seemingly unrelated disciplinary fields and thus established an open field of study that defies disciplinary boundaries.

By adopting an interdisciplinary approach, media ecology encourages a new ways of understanding the relationship between humanistic and scientific knowledge. Since media ecology relies on the systemic approaches also as a method of exploration, this approach can be recognized as an attempt to reconcile a number of disciplines in either the humanities or in scientific fields. The result of this original connection of various perspectives amount to an entirely new course of exploration and observation that successfully and transversally investigates the entire scope of human expressive forms in all of their complexity by probing a variety of side themes and related issues. The theoretical frame defined by media ecology embraces scientific disciplines such as biology, neuroscience, and cybernetics on one side and, as well, a host of humanities disciplines such as history, anthropology, psychology, or philosophy on the other side.

Finally, one more element can be recognized in media ecology as a specific and peculiar field of interdisciplinary studies: the relationship with the North American intellectual tradition of mass communication studies established around the mid twentieth century which was then later polarized around two main paradigms. One was the so-called Administrative (or Empirical) School that studied media effects from a functionalistic-quantitative perspective—in other words, it empirically reviewed the short-term impact of media-generated contents on human and social behaviour and habits. The other, the so-called Critical School, was influenced by European Marxist perspectives and studied the impact of media on human culture from a political-ideological point of view, emphasizing investigation of the causal dynamics of the media's economic control on society; an approach that was quite similar to that of the Frankfurt School. In this context, the emergence of media ecology may be interpreted as a serious and thoughtful attempt, independently made by thinkers from different disciplinary fields, to overcome the two main paradigms of the time that shared the use of a linear cause-effect logic to understand the impact of media and technology. The ecological approach can be seen as the reflection of an interest shared by scholars of many subjects, encouraging a new paradigm focused on understanding media as the indicator of social change. Rather than the opinions, concepts, or contents media convey, media ecology is concerned with the process, structure, and dynamics that rule a media environment and consequently direct its change. It is only at an ecological and environmental level—or starting from the systemic relations between human culture and its expressive forms—that the deep transformations that shape social change in any phase of human history emerge and therefore can be observed, studied and understood. From this perspective, the new paradigm of media ecology represents a seminal turning point in epistemological terms.

Interwoven issues

The body of authors, schools, and currents of thought that poured into the interdisciplinary field of media ecology can be defined as a broad catalogue of key issues and recurring concepts, the expression of an articulate and in many ways converging web of knowledge.

The first of these issues may be recognized in the relationship between technology and culture. A number of thinkers, namely Lewis Mumford (§ 2.1), Neil Postman (§ 2.3) and Jacques Ellul (§ 5.1), developed provocative meditations on the subject. A subtheme is the so-called prosthetic view of technics according to which any invention or artifact is a sort of continuation, extension, or prosthesis of human capacities. Edward Hall (§ 4.3), Marshall McLuhan (§ 3.2) and André Leroi-Gourhan (§ 5.1) emphasized this particular perspective as well.

Another line of inquiry considered the various communication forms adopted during the historical ages or phases of human culture and, specifically, the transformations they trigger in human cognitive processes. This specific area was the object of Harold Innis' analyses on so-called monopolies of knowledge (§ 3.1), as well as Walter Ong's (§ 3.3) and Jack Goody's (§ 5.3) discussions of the differences between oral and literate cultures. Ong's work offers an additional insight that can be seen as transversal to the ecological tradition and summarized in the concept of historicization of the senses, or the idea that the human sensory sphere is variously influenced by the expressive forms emerging in any historical age or culture. This specific aspect was explored, in particular, by Walter Benjamin (§ 5.2) in Europe and by Marshall McLuhan (§ 3.2) in Canada.

One more recurring element is the focus on the symbolic dimensions of human culture. This particular theoretical path was explored by Susanne Langer (§ 2.2), based on Ernst Cassirer's thought (§ 5.2), as well as by Charles Cooley's (§ 4.1) and Edward Hall's insights (§ 4.3). Langer and Hall also explored language, another key issue of media ecology, viewed as a medium that can influence the way reality is understood. Edward Sapir, Benjamin Whorf (§ 4.3), Neil Postman (§ 2.3) and the members of the so-called Cambridge School of Literary Criticism (§ 5.3) produced insights on this issue that shared similar elements on many levels.

A relational and systemic view of the communication processes is instead shared by Harold Innis (§ 3.1), Walter Ong (§ 3.3), Robert Park (§ 4.1), Gregory Bateson and the members of the Palo Alto School of Communication (§ 4.2). Finally, the contribution of Park and the members of the Chicago School of Urban Ecology reveals yet another key issue of media ecology, the focus on urban environment, previously explored by Lewis Mumford (§ 2.1) and Walter Benjamin (§ 5.2) among the others.

Intellectual historiography

It is safe to say that the intellectual history of media ecology as an actual field of study began in 1970, when, as mentioned at the beginning, Neil Postman's short paper, *The Reformed English Curriculum* (1970), formally introduced the need to create a new approach as the expression of a sensibility that was already fully explicit and ready to be officially established in academic contexts. That same year the first Media Ecology PhD program was established at New York University where Postman taught, soon to be followed by other initiatives—meetings, talks, seminars—that would attract a remarkable group of young academics who later became the core thinkers of the brand-new approach. A few years later, in the above mentioned *Teaching as a conserving activity* (1979), Postman traced a detailed map of his theoretical reference points—a list of thinkers he selected to support the new field of study, and described them as those who had actually invented the subject, «which [he had] here merely given the name "media ecology"» (p. 188). His list included some of the twentieth century's most influential intellectuals: Lewis Mumford, Harold Innis, David Riesman, Reuel Denney, Siegfried Giedion, Norbert Wiener, Edmund Carpenter, Eric Havelock, Walter Ong, Lynn White, Margaret Mead, Marshall McLuhan, Edward Hall, Joseph Weizenbaum, and Jacques Ellul.

The establishment of media ecology as a field of study happened simultaneously with another turning point in the North

American intellectual tradition. In 1971, the technology historian William Kuhns published a book that proved extremely important for the definition of the ecological paradigm. Although the phrase "media ecology" is not mentioned in *The Post-Industrial Prophets* (Kuhns, 1971), this book offers a set of brilliant insights based on the same theoretical principles that underlie media ecology. For example, he wondered: «What are the dimensions of the changes brought about by new technologies? Are the changes apparent and available to empirical studies, as the shape of cities after the automobile? Or do they tend, through their environmental presence, to be so omnipresent as to be invisible?» (p. 5). Also, the American writer presented his arguments as inspired by a pantheon of seven thinkers—Mumford, Giedion, Ellul, Innis, McLuhan, Wiener, plus the American inventor Buckminster Fuller—who, although belonging to different academic fields, partially matched the intellectual references indicated by Postman for his academic program. Kuhns' work can also be credited as the first attempt to connect authors, concepts, and approaches in order to provide the new study field with a coherent and well-defined frame and scope.

During the same years, the academic program established by Postman at New York University began to produce its first effects. In 1973, Christine Nystrom, a brilliant student of Postman's who would later become his colleague, presented the first doctoral dissertation conceived as a systematic investigation of the main interpretive elements required to understand media studies' components and environmental processes. In *Towards a Science of Media Ecology* (Nystrom, 1973), media ecology is described as a «perspective, or emerging metadiscipline, [...] broadly defined as the study of complex communication systems as environments» (p. 3), where a holistic and organic approach is applied as the main method of inquiry. Since then, many other more or less systematic studies have documented the intellectual work developed about the idea of media ecology and have recognized in the discipline the distinctive elements typical of the thought and sometimes the personality of its main proponents. In American academia, between the 1980s and the 1990s, several experts revived and actualized the work of Lewis Mumford (Carey, 1981;

Miller, 1989; Lucarelli, 1995), Siegfried Giedion (Georgiadis, 1993) and Norbert Wiener (Heims, 1980; Masani, 1980), to name just a few. In Canada, the same happened with Innis (Christian, 1980; Melody et al., 1981; Czitrom, 1982; Kroker, 1984; Carey, 1989; Stamps, 1995) and McLuhan (Kroker, 1984; Stamps, 1995; Willmott, 1996; Grosswiler, 1998; Levinson, 1999).

A second wave of historiographic contributions on this matter only came in 1998: the year that the Media Ecology Association was established. During the Association's inaugural meeting, Postman presented a sort of family tree for an approach that was already thirty years old, and at the same time pointed out the humanistic approach as the main line of development of the discipline for the future (Postman, 2000, p. 12). A few years later, in the first issue of *Explorations in Media Ecology*, the Association's official journal, Camille Paglia offered a wide-ranging review of the historical and theoretical roots of the study field that she defined as an actual North American intellectual tradition, represented by a heterogeneous group of thinkers who «creatively reshaped traditions and cross-fertilized disciplines, juxtaposing the old and new to make unexpected connections that remain fresh» (Paglia, 2002, p. 22).

Two significant works, both published in 2006, illustrated the wide variety of authors, issues, and references of media ecology as an interdisciplinary field of study. One is a well-documented introductive monograph with a detailed bibliography by Lance Strate (2006). Strate, who teaches at Fordham University in New York, is a founding member of the Media Ecology Association as well as one of the most active and influential members of the group of New York-based academicians who continue Neil Postman's intellectual legacy. The other book is a collective work edited by Casey M.K. Lum (2006)—also a founding member of the Association—with Susan Barnes, Paul Levinson, and Strate himself. The text is a collection of specialized contributions devoted to the main authors on media ecology, from Mumford to Ellul, from Innis to McLuhan, as well as the media theorist James Carey and the linguist Benjamin Lee Whorf. There are also two academic essays by Carlos Scolari (2011, 2012) that introduce key issues and authors in relation to the broader field of media studies. Two recent theoretical media and communication handbooks include a specific section on media ecology (Griffin, 2012; Massie, 2014), while a rich collection of essays (Vacker, 2015) with texts by Rushkoff, Kelly, Postman, Jenkins, and others successfully adopt an ecological view in order to develop an analysis of contemporary media phenomena. More recently, two well-detailed introductions to the field of media ecology have been authored by Dennis Cali (2017) and Lance Strate (2017).

Finally, there is the previously mentioned *Explorations in Media Ecology*, the Association's official journal and the main editorial platform for the exploration of authors, issues and analyses based on the approach of media ecology. Open to contributions of varying subjects, this journal documents the progress made by a vast community of researchers, scholars, and students who are committed to an original field of study that, almost fifty years since its establishment, has become a full-blown intellectual tradition of humanistic and interdisciplinary nature.

2. The New York School

The idea of "school" is a problematic concept in the context of academic research and even more so in general as regards the history of human knowledge. Yet, the term proves quite convenient when it is necessary to define a current of thought, an approach, a system of ideas that, although articulated and complex, are inherently coherent. I decided to adopt this expression in my book in spite of its limits and scholarly reservations, but I will use it in an informal way. On one hand, this is a way of normalizing a now mature intellectual tradition such as that of media ecology which is currently well established in several schools; on the other hand it allows me to highlight affinities and affiliations that have generated a remarkable body of ideas and concepts uniformly disseminated in twentieth-century humanistic thought that remain relevant today.

Therefore, beyond any rigid definition, the cross-disciplinary field of media ecology may be seen to incorporate several academics and thinkers who have in many cases gravitated around a common cultural environment, shared theoretical and methodological views, and sometimes even worked on the same issues concurrently. In some cases, these authors, while working in apparent isolation, were always connected to a certain Zeitgeist, an intellectual climate, a knowledge ecology that counted more than the individual research trajectories. The sum of these authors' impact can only be appreciated across time and through a rigorous survey overviewing the overall academic and theoretical enterprise of these thinkers. Attempting to systematize this intellectual tradition requires a re-reading and re-assessment of the heritage of some important twentieth century thinkers in order to find in each of them one or more elements to support a theoretical project, a methodology, a vision that in many ways can only be embraced in its entirety and formal articulations in hindsight.

New York's intellectual environment can certainly be considered the epicentre of media ecology; a centre around which a group of key figures, with different and complementary roles, were active particularly within some of the top-tier universities based in the American metropolis. Their roles can be determined as follows. First of all, the pioneers, initiators or forerunners such as Lewis Mumford (§ 2.1) and Susanne Langer (§ 2.2), who will be the subjects of the following chapters. The works of these two authors emerged as a foundational bedrock for a later generation of New York-based intellectuals, an interpretive key that could be used, developed, and updated to consolidate their approach, which is what Neil Postman (§ 2.3) did when he successfully consolidated the attempt to define and name a new field of study.

A strong and charismatic personality, Postman also took the role of the leader who often justified the more or less formal existence of the school of thought. As a leader, he successfully catalyzed academic attention, provided stimuli to the emerging field, and disseminated ideas by using all the leverage he had from his membership in the National Council of Teachers of English, in a commission charged to reform the American school system, to his teaching post at the New York University, and finally, to the intense educational activities he developed as a talented author and brilliant lecturer. He also created a closely knit network of connections and promoted synergies with intellectuals and thinkers of the New York intellectual scene, such as Louis Forsdale, John Culkin, Charles Weingartner, Henry Perkinson, Tony Schwartz, Gary Gumpert, Paul Ryan (Strate, 2006, p. 55; Gencarelli, 2006, p. 91). In addition, he intercepted the innovative impact of the ideas developed by another so-called school, the Toronto School, and grafted them onto the cultural scene of his own city. Finally, Postman inspired and trained a host of students who went on to establish the third generation of academics, in doing so nurturing an intellectual heritage that is still alive and well in New York: the birthplace of media ecology.

2.1 Lewis Mumford and the ecology of technics

Lewis Mumford (1895-1990) is a key figure in the intellectual roots of media ecology within American academia. Due to his considerable influence on a remarkable group of authors, many of them based in New York, Mumford may be considered as one of the earliest propagators, if not the initiator of the New York School.

An author who defied definition, though seemingly related to the North-American pragmatist tradition, over his long career Lewis Mumford proved himself as a full-range thinker: a prolific essayist and writer, a journalist and historian who could read his changing times, an architectural, art and literature critic, the author of a remarkable body of studies on the city, a forerunner of a global approach to urban issues, so much so that he became a true authority in this field. The richness and undying relevance of his thought are widely recognized, mainly because he anticipated issues and questions that are still very much with us. Many of his texts are still considered cornerstones of urban planning literature.

Born in Flushing, a small town in the county of Queens, Mumford spent his entire intellectual life in New York. His fascination of the metropolitan landscape, a melting pot of architectural styles and diverse cultures, combined with the sparkling cultural scene of New York inspired in Mumford a special and devoted connection with the urban centre which was additionally nurtured by long contemplative walks through the city. That feeling was so strong that he even considered himself, beyond his family relations, as the offspring of a place like no other in the world, a «child of Manhattan» (Mumford, 1982, p. 25). His multiple interests in sociology, philosophy, engineering, and urban planning propelled him through a complicated course of study in early life. In 1919 he attended a series of lessons at an independent institute, the New School for Social Research, where he came in touch with several professors including the economist, Thorstein Veblen, who was previously one of the key intellectuals of the Chicago scene. Veblen would have a lasting impact on Mumford's socio-economic views (Halton, 1995; Lucarelli, 1995; Diggins, 1999), in particular concerning the European *milieu* developed around thinkers like Marx and Weber (Li, 2009). Although he never got a college degree, Mumford still emerged as a brilliant and original scholar who contributed to several influential sociology, literature, and architecture journals, and taught at several American universities including Columbia, Stanford, and the University of Pennsylvania. In April 1938 he received the honour of being featured on the cover of "Time" magazine. He also received several awards and honorary degrees from the most influential institutions in the US and Europe.

One of the most significant encounters in his life, when he was barely in his twenties, was with the Scottish biologist **Patrick Geddes** (1854-1932; § 5.3) whose ideas were particularly appreciated by the intellectuals of the time. With his syncretic approach to urban planning and sociology based on anthropological, religious, and economic concerns, Geddes was indeed one of the first scholars to address the complexity of the relations between human and natural environments, promoting from a sociological perspective the concept of "human ecology" (Geddes, 1915; Meller, 1990): a concept that had been introduced a few years earlier by the American biologist Ellen Richards (1907) and would be later developed by some members of the Chicago School (McKenzie, 1925; Park, 1936; Wirth, 1945; § 4.1). Mumford became one of the most enthusiastic followers of Geddes and his ecological view of human culture as well as his devoted disciple. In all of his numerous autobiographical writings, Mumford never neglected to pay homage to Geddes and declare himself in debt to him (Miller, 1989), a gratitude that is also documented by a prolific correspondence (Novak, 1995). The ecological view acquired by his brilliant mentor would therefore be a constant influence across the entire life of this scholar and intellectual.

Mumford's production as an author is quite vast: his roughly thirty books and over one thousand articles demonstrate an uncommon ability to combine diverse issues and themes in a complex and articulated manner based on a hybrid scientific/humanistic approach (Hughes and Hughes, 1990). On the other hand, his brilliant prose and accessible language reflect an openly generalist approach to knowledge used to overcome academic or disciplinary specialism and provide a comprehensive view of human, global, organic, and especially cross-disciplinary issues.

In *The Story of Utopias* (1922), a book written during his youth, Mumford already expressed this peculiar approach that reflected the deep influence of his mentor Patrick Geddes, and openly contrasted the division applied to human issues in civilized societies with their classification in separate specialist contexts. What Mumford tried to articulate in this fascinating review of the history of utopias—or «the other half of the Story of Mankind» (p. 9)—is the so-called utopian method: «looking at life by considering all of it simultaneously and seeing it as an interrelated whole: not as a casual mix but as an organic system of parts that can have a better organization, where balance should be maintained, like in a living organism, in order to promote growth and progress» (p. 4, preface to the 1962 edition).

Technics and Civilization

The four books Mumford wrote considering the modern human condition in a clearly new perspective constitute the central core of his overall oeuvre. Ambitiously titled *The Renewal of Life* overall, these works follow a coherent and programmatic plan, and include *Technics and Civilization* (1934), *The Culture of Cities* (1938), *The Condition of Man* (1944) and *The Conduct of Life* (1951).

The first book, *Technics and Civilization* (1934), is considered a seminal text in the history of technology and of the relationships between technology and culture. Mumford draws from Geddes a peculiar periodization of the evolution of Western civilization and its historical ages based on the main phases of technological innovation rather than the succession of kingdoms and dynasties, conflicts, doctrines, or ideologies. He chose this approach in order to consider the cultural forms of human civilization in light of the deep changes introduced by the development of *technics*, which is why the history of technology and the history of human culture are clearly interconnected. Mumford used the word technics, quite unusual at the time, rather than the more common term technology, specifically to embrace all the aspects of human culture—not just material expressive forms—considering operational knowledge layered in time through both technological and social processes. In particular, his goal was to shed a light on the origin of the so-called machine age and to view the development of technics not as a closed system but rather as an element of human culture connected to it. He clearly stated this goal in the opening pages of the book: «The world of technics is not isolated and self-contained: it reacts to forces and impulses that come from apparently remote parts of the environment» (p. 6). Therefore, although Mumford gave technics a relevant role, he interpreted its effects in the context of a complex systems of feedback, that concurrently involved social practices, human lifestyles, habits, and behaviours. He describes this feedback as a «process of technical syncretism» (p. 107), or as a synergy between the individual parts, the result of which is more than their sum. Such process is based on the complexity of the relations between the realm of technics, which is ultimately always the expression of a knowledge, and the realm of human culture considered as a coherent and unitary system. In other words, more so than the technological features of each age, what really counts is the general system of social and cultural forms of that age. This is once more a holistic and organic view applied to the study of relationships between technics and culture, summarized as follows: «It is the whole, the *gestalt* of cultural history, that Mumford wants to convey» (Kuhns, 1971, p. 33).

Mumford sees the evolution of the so-called mechanical age, the human age dominated by automation and mechanistic production, as divided into three major phases; three «successive but over-lapping and interpenetrating phases» (Mumford, 1934, p. 109). Two of these are explicitly borrowed from Geddes, who demonstrated that industrial civilization should be viewed as comprised of two separate and successive phases of human history rather than as one single process. First, there is the so-called *paleotechnic* phase that started with the first industrial revolution and the introduction of the steam engine around 1750. Second, there is the *neotechnic* phase, more-or-less corresponding to the second industrial revolution, starting with the beginning of electricity in the late nineteenth century and the propagation of electric technology in the early twentieth century. Mumford adds one more phase to the two periods of industrial civilization described by Geddes—the *eotechnic* phase, or the period of preparation of industrial age that roughly stretched from the High Middle Ages to the first industrial revolution and was therefore a long gestation of the modern age. This addition is based on one of the peculiar insights of the New York-based thinker. Rather than recognizing in the invention of the steam engine the defining innovation of the industrial civilization and its social organization, Mumford's consideration reaches back several centuries to the age of medieval monasteries. The structured and strictly organized life of the monastic system was viewed by him as the dawn of a new kind of rational organization of society based on serial production and a regular rhythm of the day. The technical invention that was at the base of this system promoted an irreversible change in the perception of time. Indeed, the mechanical clock «has been the foremost machine in modern technics. [...] the key-machine of the modern industrial era. [...] a piece of power-machinery whose *product* is seconds and minutes: by its essential nature it dissociated time from human events» (pp. 14-15). Therefore, the concept of abstract and quantifiable time created a new perceptual and cognitive environment for humankind, a new vision of space and time made of measurable sequences that had to be filled, used, saved; a syncretic environment from which the modern forms of social organization and the future innovations of the industrial age would grow.

More particularly, as Mumford explains, each of these phases, besides defining a period of human history, corresponds to a «technological complex», or a system of material factors such as the use of certain raw materials—water, wind and wood in the eotechnic phase, iron and coal in the paleotechnic phase, electricity and metal alloys in the more recent neotechnic phase—that become involved with a series of cultural factors such as social and work conditions, or the development of knowledge. The connection of these factors within a technological complex is such that each of its parts «symbolizes a whole series of relationships within that complex» (p. 130). Therefore, technics can be seen as the vibrant and organic expression of human culture, and not as its mere instrument. Human beings ourselves are the result of a slow layering of habits, beliefs, and tendencies that shows how technological innovation is nothing but the reflection of a dynamic interaction between human beings and their environment. All this ultimately reveals the humanistic approach adopted by Mumford and the ecological perspective inspired by Geddes constantly reflected therein. These idiosyncratic aspects of his work promoted Mumford's work as a major contributor in the construction of a new understanding of urban order.

The city as a medium

In the second book of the series, *The Culture of Cities* (1938), Mumford approaches the dynamic interaction between culture and technics in light of the relationships between human condition and the city, viewed as an ideal environment for the development of cultural and social systems. The city as a theme would be explored further in a successive work that many consider as the peak of Mumford's opus, and as such became a classic for urban studies, *The City in History* (1961): a long historiographic review, an enthralling narrative of how Western cities evolved from the Middle Ages to the contemporary age. The approach that underlies the intellectual tradition of media ecology is brilliantly encapsulated in the well-known incipit of the book: «This book opens with a city that was, symbolically, a world: it closes with a world that has become, in many practical aspects, a city» (p. XI). The city provides indeed one of the best instruments to understand the role of technics as an environment created by the human beings where they work and live.

For Mumford, the city itself is and expression of human evolution, the result of humanity's slow and constant action on its own environment aimed at adapting it to our own needs in terms of safety, stability, management of goods, etc. At the same time, though, it becomes a new environment for humanity, in the sense that it can spark new needs and social and cultural issues in our way of perceiving and thinking about the world. Mumford, according to Geddes, saw the city as «the specialized organ of social transmission» (Mumford, 1938, p. XXVII), the most explicit expression of human civilization, the result of an ecological and social balance. In his words, the environmental role played by the urbanization processes on human culture has a major impact: «Through its concentration of physical and cultural power, the city heightened the tempo of human intercourse and translated its products into forms that could be stored and reproduced. Through its monuments, written records, and orderly habits of association, the city enlarged the scope of all human activities, extending them backwards and forwards in time. [...] the city became capable of transmitting a complex culture from generation to generation, for it marshaled together not only the physical means but human agents needed to pass on and enlarge this heritage. That remains the greatest of the city's gifts. As compared with the complex human order of the city, our present ingenious electronic mechanisms for storing and transmitting information are crude and limited» (1961, p. 569).

Mumford considered the city as a medium (Kittler, 1996); the urban environment is viewed as an ecological process that can give human experience a unified meaning. This deep sense of unitarity and consistency can be found in *The Culture of Cities*: «Mind takes form in the city; and in turn, urban forms condition mind» (1938, p. XV). This can be described as a pedagogical function of the urban environment, the expression of the deep connection humans have with the past and the foundation of his historical identity. The city as an educating environment is the place where human experience is shaped by the interaction with the world of technics. The brilliant words that close *The City in History* reflect an auspice that perhaps rises above the most optimistic expectations: «The chief function of the city is to convert power into form, energy into culture, dead matter into the living symbols of art, biological reproduction into social creativity» (Mumford, 1961, p. 571).

Megamachine and human environment

The works that followed the cycle of *The Renewal of Life*—in particular *Art and Technics* (1952), *The Transformations of Man* (1956) and the two-books *The Myth of the Machine* (1967; 1970)—show a slow but clear change of focus (Carey, 1981). Having witnessed the disasters of the Second World War—during which he lost his first son who fought with the Allied troops in Italy—including Nazi extermination camps and the horror of the atomic bomb, Mumford would lower his optimistic expectations towards the potential of technological progress as the key of an integration between humans and their environment in terms of a virtuous use of natural and human resources. The tragic international events of those years led him to recognize the unlucky return of what he began to define as a "megamachine" (Mumford, 1967, p. 317; Latouche, 1995), or the coercive aspect of technological, cultural, and social development. In the past of human civilization, the megamachine had already emerged as a sort of invisible force that could mobilize huge masses of individuals—as its unwitting cogs—and huge quantities of materials, in order to build the works or endeavours that were required to exert social power. In human history, from the pyramids in ancient Egypt to the administrative-military apparatus of the Roman empire, the megamachine had certainly expanded the power of those empires but at the same time had led them to implode. Having reached this insight, Mumford warned against the contemporary megamachine and the out-of-control propelling power it had acquired, the effects of which were now clearly visible both in the organization of the armies during WWII and in the totalitarian structure of the former Soviet Union, eventually in the ever increasing nuclear arms race, and in the so-called world environmental crisis.

In time, Mumford would become a relentless critic of a certain economic, military, and scientific élite that put itself at the service of the logics of destruction and violence against humanity and the environment. The contemporary megamachine propels individuals and technologies by silently penetrating several fields of human organization. He indicates five factors—politics, energy, productivity, profit, publicity—as a "pentagon of power" (Mumford, 1970) that not only reveals a clear reference to the American political-military complex, but hints at a remarkably larger crisis of conscience that affects the entire and complex system of Western society.

The accusations of intellectual militancy Mumford directs towards the *intelligentsia* of the time is actually a reflection of the honest humanism that constantly guided his long and brilliant critical adventure. And the humanistic approach is actually the solution Mumford proposed to address the coercive action of an invisible power, the megamachine, that effectively reduced the human beings to mere cogs. It is as though he never abandoned the direction he had taken ever since his early work, *The Story of Utopias* (Mumford, 1922). This time, the opening to a utopian dream, the other half of a not completely written story, appears as an inalienable necessity to contemporary humanity: overcoming the self-deception of technological progress seen as an independent, unstoppable, or uncontrollable power. Mumford writes: «Since machines are an enigma, they offer no explanation. The answer to this enigma is in the nature of man» (1944, p. 137), which means considering human as part of change, a change «that should go *towards* the individual. Without that change, no great betterments will take place in the social order. Once that change begins, everything is possible» (p. 514).

The trail blazed by Mumford that continues to be the path of media ecology implies the recognition of the complex and dynamic balance that involves both human beings and the environment in a sort of "ecology of technics" (Strate, Lum, 2000), or an organic harmony between the renewal of humanity and technological innovation that the young and brilliant son of New York would never stop pursuing in his utopian dream. Unsurprisingly, his inherent power of conjuring a new and positive course of events for the development of human culture made him become one of the main inspirations for American ecological thought. Therefore, it is ecology of technics shaped by Mumford's thought, that can be seen to inspire a new holistic and global awareness of the great social, cultural, and technological issues of our time.

Lewis Mumford's main works
The Story of Utopias (1922)
Technics and Civilization (1934)
The Culture of Cities (1938)
The Condition of Man (1944)
The Conduct of Life (1951)
Art and Technics (1952)
In the Name of Sanity (1954)
The Transformations of Man (1956)
The City in History (1961)

The Myth of the Machine: Vol. I (1967)
The Myth of the Machine: Vol. II (1970)
Sketches from Life: The Autobiography of Lewis Mumford (1982)

Further readings
Carey J.W. (1981), "McLuhan and Mumford: The Roots of Modern Media Analysis", Journal of Communication, 31, 3, pp.162-168.
Hughes T.P, Hughes A.C., eds.(1990), *Lewis Mumford: Public Intellectual*, Oxford University Press, New York.
Li S. (2009), *Lewis Mumford. Critic of Culture and Civilization*, Peter Lang, Bern.
Lucarelli M. (1995), *Lewis Mumford and the Ecological Region*, Guilford, New York.
Miller D.L. ed. (1986), *The Lewis Mumford Reader*, Pantheon Books, New York.
Miller D.L. (1989), *Lewis Mumford: A Life*, Weidenfeld & Nicolson, New York.
Novak F.G., ed. (1995), *Lewis Mumford and Patrick Geddes. The correspondence*, Routledge, London.
Strate L., Lum C.M.K. (2000), "Lewis Mumford and the Ecology of Technics", The New Jersey Journal of Communication, 8, 1, pp. 56-78.
Stunkel K.R. (2004), *Understanding Lewis Mumford: A guide for the perplexed*, Edwin Mellen Press, New York.

2.2 Susan Langer and the ecology of forms

Another major author emerged out of New York academia, specifically out of the discipline of philosophy, with a work that is still considered as a primary reference for the definition of the intellectual roots of media ecology in North American contexts. This is the American philosopher Susanne K. Langer (1895-1985).

A brilliant scholar, an expert in modern logic and symbolic thought who could easily and originally move between theory of knowledge, cognitive anthropology, art, aesthetics, and philosophy of the mind, Susanne Langer was one of the first women to successfully develop a career in the international philosophical scene. Her intellectual legacy interprets the expressive forms of human culture—media viewed in a wider meaning—in their symbolic dimension. Therefore, media would be like symbolic environments within which the peculiar attitudes and experiences of human culture are defined. Developed as a well thought-out and coherent theoretical corpus that successfully transcends disciplinary specialism while preserving a firm foundation in its methodological principles, the work of the American scholar was developed over sixty years and provided media ecology with a philosophical and epistemological foundation rooted in the truest North American pragmatist tradition and at the same time nurtured by several relevant European influences. Her research provides a firm conceptual framework that is particularly well-suited to the systemic approach adopted by media ecology that in this sense may be viewed as an ecology of human culture considered from its symbolic dimension, or even as an ecology of the human mind viewed in light of the relations and interaction of organism and environment.

Langer was born in New York, the daughter of German immigrants. Even as a young girl, she showed a keen passion for literature and music, as well as a strong attraction for philosophical studies: at twelve years of age when she already played the cello and the piano, she had written a book of short stories and read Kant's *Critique of Pure Reason* (Dryden, 2003). She followed her entire course of studies at the Radcliffe College, the Harvard Annex for women, first under Henry Sheffer, when she specialized in formal logic, philosophy of language, and gnoseology, and then with Alfred North Whitehead, who would easily recognize the uncommon talent of that young and brilliant student. Upon receiving her doctorate in 1926, she started collaborating first with influential philosophical journals, and then became a teacher at Radcliffe College; she would keep that post until 1942, when she would go back to New York to teach at the University of New York and at Columbia, as well as at other universities in the US as a visiting professor. Finally, she became a professor at the University of Connecticut in 1954. Another important influence in her academic career, besides Sheffer and Whitehead in Harvard (Dryden, 1997), was the German philosopher Ernst Cassirer (§ 5.2), whom she met in Yale in 1941, and who would have a remarkable impact on her research on the vast realm of the expressive elements of human culture defined by the well-known expression of "symbolic forms" (Cassirer, 1923-29). Over her long career, she received several major awards including many honorary degrees. The wide publicity her works enjoyed (the Susanne K. Langer Papers including her manuscripts and letters are now at the Houghton Library in Harvard) and their exceptional success within the field of philosophic studies in the international context reflect the enormous influence of her intellectual legacy.

The central core of Langer's thought is recognizable in three major works, each in its own way aimed at overcoming the analytic approach that, in the first half of the twentieth century and inspired by European empiricism and logic positivism, was pushing American philosophic research to adopt an analytic and objectifying attitude towards the facts of knowledge by relying on the methodological strictness typical of scientific research. In this context, the Langer's theoretical contribution can certainly be viewed as original and in a certain way revolutionary, as it aimed at overcoming the rigid opposition between the idea of an external world objectively accessible to knowledge through the analytic method and the idea of an inner world that cannot be controlled by knowledge due to its unfathomable subjective dimensions. In other words, Langer's work addresses the complexity of the processes that shape human knowledge and experience by overcoming the dichotomies—mind vs. body, nature vs. culture, spirit vs. matter, reason vs. instinct—deeply rooted in the modernist philosophical tradition and still present in the analytic approach. Langer's entire philosophic project was therefore developed around a new method of inquiry aimed at conceiving the interaction between human beings and their environment in terms of complementariness, coexistence, belonging to the same horizon of sense. Such approach opens new possibilities for the logic-formal study of experience that, although not resulting in an immediate scientific-natural proof, can be defined as essential in terms of the construction of the structure of human culture in its entirety.

The symbolic turning-point

Langer's first two books—written when she was still studying at the Radcliffe College—are *A Logical Analysis of Meaning* (1930), with an introductory note by Alfred North Whitehead, where she addresses the meaning of philosophic interpretation, and *An In-*

troduction to Symbolic Logic (1937), a systematic guide to logic-formal thought applied to symbolic language. But it was *Philosophy in a New Key* (1942), dedicated to Whitehead, that—with over half million copies sold all over the world—earned Langer a place in contemporary philosophy due to the focus on the peculiar element of human cognitive activity, the *passe-partout* that would transversally run through her entire intellectual production: the symbolic dimension of human culture.

The conceptual core of the text is indeed the human need to symbolize. The "new key" is the understanding of the development of human thought through the need to invent meanings, add levels of meaning to the forms of experience, transform these into symbols, or give experience a conceptual, abstract, or symbolic, meaning. The symbolizing ability of human beings is seen, therefore, as the cornerstone of a new gnoseologic paradigm, a new approach in the interpretation of the entire meaning of human experience, a structural principle of the construction of experience that builds the relationship of human beings with the world. With *Philosophy in a New Key*, the linguistic turning point that is typical of twentieth-century philosophy acquires the features of a true symbolic turning point, insofar as language itself is viewed as a particular and specific expression of the symbolizing ability that generally characterizes the biunique relationship between human organism and environment. The symbolic turning point achieved by the American scholar in terms of the meaning that should be given to the structures of experience and knowledge in relation with human expressive form, linguistic or otherwise, is indeed the result of a sophisticated process of confluence between two peculiar features of the American logic-symbolic tradition and of the European neo-Kantian tradition. Therefore, Langer's thought represents an interesting synthesis of two wide-ranging philosophic systems: Ernst Cassirer's philosophy of symbolic forms (§ 5.2) and William James' pragmatism, as well as a general confluence between the American development of British New Criticism, as represented by Ivor Richards (§ 5.3), and the view of European phenomenology, as represented by Edmund Husserl. Langer's system can be seen as the link between European and American traditions, the fundamental underpinnings of logic and philosophical meditation within media ecology.

Langer's grafting of Cassirer's philosophy of symbolic forms onto the North-American intellectual endeavours, and in particular the field of knowledge theory, is functional in making the phenomenological analysis of the relationship between perception and knowledge, which is typical of the philosophy of culture illustrated by Cassirer in Europe (Skidelsky, 2008), converge with the research conducted in the US by Peirce, Carnap, Morris in the wide field of emerging theories of signification and semiotic/semiology theory.

Cassirer's teaching is therefore the background of the arguments developed by Susanne Langer, effectively an effort to capture the unitary meaning of philosophical study starting from the multiple and diversified expressive forms of human culture, especially in light of its unavoidable specificity: the use of symbols. Symbolic activity is the peculiar element that leads humans to build the specifically human substrate that is culture: Cassirer's definition of human species as *animal symbolicum* is well-known (1944). Indeed, the symbolic form transcends the perceptual sphere due to the shaping action promoted by the cultural environment, an ecology of symbols, interpretations and meanings that gives human experience an always new and evolving structure. According to Cassirer, the symbolic nature is shared by the different expressions of human culture—language, myth, religion, art, and therefore media in their broader meaning—where these appear as elements of a mutually formative process. In other words, they are shaped by the symbolizing drive that is typical of human thought, but at the same time they act as elements that can shape additional levels of symbolization. The evolution of human experience can be inscribed in the same process of symbolic formation illustrated by Cassirer: human beings shape their cultural forms and symbols, and at the same time are shaped by them. Therefore, unlike what happens in the animal realm, the meaning humans attribute to the inner experience of the knowledge of the world is defined by the symbolic dimension of the environment in which they inhabit. Once the symbols are formed, or once a shared cultural form is established of them, they help to define a vision of the world that shapes the very perception of reality. In other words, the cultural environment of humans and the system of expressive forms through which it develops define the gnosiological assumption that gives meaning to the human experience of interaction and interpretation of the world, the key of which lies precisely in the formation, adoption, and interpretation of symbols. Langer writes: «In the fundamental notion of symbolization – mythical, practical, or mathematical, it makes no difference – we have the keynote of all humanistic problems. In it lies a new conception of "mentality", that may illumine questions of life and consciousness, instead of obscuring them as traditional "scientific methods" have done» (Langer, 1942, p. 25).

On a strictly humanistic level, in an attempt to overcome the rigidity of scientific, analytic paradigms, the symbolizing ability argued by Langer appears as a peculiar activity of the human mind that promotes the particular formative process established by the interaction of human beings with the environment. Such activity transcends reasoning or the linguistic code of experience. Further on, she writes: «Man's conquest of the world undoubtedly rests on the supreme development of his brain, which allows him to synthesize, delay, and modify his reactions by the interpolation of *symbols* in the gaps and confusions of direct experience, and by means of "verbal signs" to add the experiences of other people to his own» (p. 29). The concept of symbol Langer proposes is therefore wider, and not exclusively connected to language in general and to logic-formal language in particular. Symbolic activity appears rather as a starting point for any human experience and, in particular, for the interpretive experiences shaped by imagination, creative thinking, the processes of daydreaming, when the act of perception is nothing but the result of the operation of transformation—the attribution of a form—and constant connection to a cultural dimension that is typical of human symbolizing ability.

The perceptual universe is contiguous to the horizon of experience defined by the symbolic dimension that underlies the human cultural environment. In other words, the symbolizing ability literally shapes experience as any instance of human action occurs within a symbolic and therefore cultural environment. Experience and its inherent cognitive ability are processed within this environment. In all this lies an actual ecology of experience—a key notion of North American pragmatist tradition—that finds its habitat in the symbolic dimension.

Between feeling and form

As we have seen, the key concept of symbol in its cognitive and cultural dimension underlies Susanne Langer's most successful book. But, another essential element is integrated therein and further completes her intellectual survey and projects the symbolic dimension of human culture as an organic and continuous system (Barilli, 1961), as such perfectly in sync with the theoretical foundation of media ecology. This is the notion of form: the subject of *Feeling and Form* (1953), that she dedicated to Ernst Cassirer. Form, in this sense, is what can give a peculiar meaning to the structures of human perception. Langer reached this conclusion as the result of a wider meditation in order to «reinforce the philosophical and scientific foundation of aesthetic experience» (Gardner, 1982, p. 54). In Langer's aesthetics, the form of sensible knowledge, or the complex meaning structure within which human beings interact with the world, is not conceived as a mere expression of content, or as the reflection of a series of exchanges that originate in human experience. The structural and formal level of knowledge is also seen as having a particular formative function, as it can influence choices, habits, and attitudes that give human experience a meaning not strictly related to logic-linguistic functions but rather connected to the particular cognitive system that is typical of human beings in their cultural dimension. That is, once more, the symbolizing ability that frames the complex process of human culture.

In *Feeling and Form* (1953), Langer recognized that a group of expressive forms including art, music, and poetry most transparently reveal the symbolic mechanism that defines the relationship between human beings and the world. The issue of sensorial *feeling* has a central role in Langer's work, and such it is discussed in the collection of lectures, *Problems of Art* (1957), and in the collection of essays, *Philosophical Sketches* (1962): both educational works and as such easily accessible to a non specialized readership. In the terminology adopted by Langer, language is recognized as a way, albeit a particular one, of symbolizing the world. As a form of discursive symbolicity, or one that uses a conventional system of signs and codes, an arbitrary and selective correspondence, decided preemptively and basically univocal in terms of form and meaning, it is also called representational symbolicity. The focus on language should therefore be complemented by an analysis of not purely linguistic forms that Langer's system of thought places in the realm of presentational—neither discursive, nor linguistic—symbolicity that can convey the continuity, analogy, and direct similarity between form and meaning.

In Langer's vision, the inherently discursive quality of language fails to convey the symbolic dimension of the human emotional sphere, while other expressive forms—such as art—have a presentational, analog, immediate character that acts on the forms of perceptual and sensorial experience. In other words, «the ways in which language cuts up and reassembles the world are not the same as the ways in which we experience the world through our senses» (Nystrom, 2006, p. 298). We need symbolic presentational forms because language fails to intercept the aspects of experience we mainly perceive through the senses. Whereas language reproduces a mediated experience by simplifying the wide range of phenomena in human feeling, art forms facilitate an immediate knowledge and therefore convey many symbolic aspects of human culture just as they are, presented without filters and in their entirety. Langer writes: «The import of an art symbol cannot be built up like the meaning of a discourse, but must be seen *in toto* first; that is, the "understanding" of a work of art begins with an intuition of the whole presented feeling [...]. Artistic import, unlike verbal meaning, can only be exhibited, not demonstrated to anyone to whom the art symbol is not lucid» (Langer, 1953, p. 379). With this, Langer recognizes that both discursive and presentational symbolicity play a role, although in a different and complementary way, in creating the array of knowledge, emotions, thoughts and feelings that is the foundation of human experience. Langer actually «aims at transforming Kant's epistemological thought from epistemology of perception and concept into epistemology of medium and form» (Innis R.E., 2009, p. 46). In other words, the symbolic forms of human culture, or the formal structure of the processes of discursivity and symbolic presentation used by human beings, directly influence the content of representation. This is actually a sort of philosophical legitimization of McLuhan's statement "the medium is the message" (Strate, 2006, p. 84), one of media ecology's key arguments (§ 3.2).

The feeling-form dualism is thus resolved, establishing between the two terms a bond of a symbolic type, a close connection that fully mirrors the subject-object relationship. By transforming experience into symbols, and by giving the symbolic dimension of culture a form, or a medium, Susanne Langer's work once more effectively points at the symbolizing ability as the peculiar feature that makes human beings so different from other animals. Also, feeling, that results from an animal-related biological process, reaches in the human being its highest and most intense peak, as the array of expressive forms and their creative, productive and cognitive processes—the expressions of human culture's typical symbolizing ability—clearly show. In other words, the act of feeling is viewed as a symbolic form of knowledge influenced by the symbolic components that are typical of the cultural dimension.

Mind and knowledge

Mind. An Essay on Human Feeling (1967-82) was the trilogy that completed Langer's wide-ranging intellectual achievement and finally offers a comprehensive picture of what can be defined as an actual philosophy of the mind (Powers, 2006) aimed at understanding the development of human thought through the lens of the symbolic activity that projects it as such, or as an anthropological and phylogenetic survey that proposes the symbolizing function as the element that is typical of human relationship with reality. This implies several affinities between Langer's theory of the mind and the dynamics of systems theory (Shelley, 1998) developed a few years afterwards. With *Mind,* Langer actually developed a fully-fledged anthropological theory of human ethics (Powers, 2006, p. 312) based on a reconstruction of the main evolutionary phases of the system of symbolic values that underlie cultural processes, a sort of natural history of the mind from animism to magism, from religious thought to the scientific thought. While *Feeling and Form* (1953) analyzed the clear distinction between discursive and presentational symbolicity, the focus here is the conceptual field of sensorial and cognitive experience. Langer explores *feeling* in its widest meaning, in every form of human production, and not just in the specifically artistic production. This fundamental shift effectively places Langer's thought at the roots of media ecology. The sensorial and cognitive experience that underlies the relationship human beings have with the world, in its historical and cultural development, should indeed be considered as the result of a symbolic process developed at the cultural level: a complex system of values that is in many ways imperceptible. In other words, this is an actual symbolic environment, an ecology of forms where media—the entirety of human expressive forms—play an essential role in creating habits, concepts, beliefs so deeply rooted that they become the experiential bedrock of any social and cultural activity, the sensorial and cognitive background of human actions that it provides with an indefinite, although limited, number of possible ways of building a symbolic relationship with reality.

Susanne Langer's main works
A Logical Analysis of Meaning (1930)
An Introduction to Symbolic Logic (1937)
Philosophy in a New Key (1942)
Feeling and Form (1953)
Problems of Art (1957)
Philosophical Sketches (1962)
Mind. An Essay on Human Feeling, 3 voll. (1967-82)

Further readings
Innis, R.E. (2009), *Susanne Langer in Focus*, Indiana University Press, Bloomington.
Nystrom C. (2006), "Symbols, Thought, and 'Reality'. The Contributions of Benjamin Lee Whorf and Susanne K. Langer to Media Ecology", in Lum C.M.K., ed. *Perspectives on Culture, Technology and Communication: The Media Ecology Tradition*, Hampton Press, Cresskill, NJ, pp. 275-301.
Powers J.H. (2006), "Susanne Langer's Philosophy of Mind. Some implications for Media Ecology", in Lum C.M.K., ed., *Perspectives on Culture, Technology and Communication: The Media Ecology Tradition*, Hampton Press, Cresskill, NJ, pp. 303-334.
Shelley C. (1998), "Consciousness, Symbols and Aesthetics. A Jast-so Story and its Implications in Susanne Langer's Mind", *Philosophical-Psychology*, 11, 1, pp. 45-66.

2.3 Neil Postman and media education

Neil Postman (1931-2003) should be recognized more than anyone else for establishing media ecology as a field of study in North American academic contexts. As mentioned before (§ 1.1), he came up with the definition that, since the late nineteen-sixties, has begun to circulate in the wide realm of North American media and communication studies along with a new concern for the expressive forms of human culture and a new understanding of the media in their systemic, relational, environmental dimension. His was a quite specific approach that viewed the "media as environments" (Postman, 1970, p. 161), or was more generally aimed at understanding «the ways in which the interaction between media and human beings give a culture its character and, one might say, help a culture to maintain symbolic balance» (2000, p. 62).

Besides coining the term media ecology and repeatedly explaining its meaning in connection with culture, technology, and communication, Postman should also be credited as the scholar who explicitly pointed out some of its intellectual roots, recognizing a long list of thinkers—mainly from the North-American tradition, although he was careful to point at some important European connections—in order to develop the new field of study from a firm theoretical, methodological, and, in some ways, also critical foundation. For these reasons, Postman's work is a key reference for whoever wants to approach media ecology, both in its original and comprehensive articulation and in connection with the field of study that Postman considered as a testing ground for an intellectual challenge of a more humanistic nature: education.

A particularly prolific author, a talented essayist, a gifted public speaker, as well a critic who carefully observed the cultural phenomena of his time, Postman conducted his research from the vast field of pedagogy and the study of educational systems. His concern for education and learning processes led him to explore the development of linguistic and communication forms through the lens of media. For this reason among others, Postman is not just the creator of media ecology—he is also one of the most original pioneers of *media education*, a field that studies media from a pedagogical perspective (Buckingham, 2003; Fraser and Wardle, 2013).

Born in New York, where he spent his entire intellectual career, Neil Postman began to study English language and literature at the State University at Fredonia, and subsequently studied linguistics and pedagogy at Columbia University in New York City, under the mentorship of Louis Forsdale (1922-1999). An influential professor at that famous university and a pioneer of the study of the relationships between culture and communication, Forsdale is the author of *Perspectives on Communication* (Forsdale, 1981), still considered a seminal text of the so-called New York School. During the summer of 1955, Forsdale himself introduced his young student to Marshall McLuhan, who was then in New York for a series of summer seminars at Columbia (1989). Since those early meetings, McLuhan's charisma, ideas, and works deeply influenced Postman's intellectual development and a relationship of mutual appreciation started to form between the two men. In 1959, Postman was appointed at the New York University, where he would teach for his entire career and began original research through different disciplinary fields that would effectively combine different approaches within a unique theoretical-critical and at the same time practical project. This original approach is what keeps his ideas enduringly relevant today.

The languages of media

A prolific writer, Postman authored or co-authored about thirty books as well as approximately one hundred essays. In addition to his extensive bibliography, numerous TV appearances as well as a number of interviews and talks testify to his charisma and brilliant gift as an educator. Over the years, Postman conducted his research over multiple fronts.

His first book, *Television and the Teaching of English* (1961), was commissioned by the National Council of Teachers of English upon Forsdale's suggestion and provides a well-organized introduction to his entire intellectual enterprise (Gencarelli, 2006). It is an in-depth analysis of the impact of the newly born TV medium was already having, or might have, on the American educational system and on the forms of language and literature of the time. The critical focus on a mass medium like TV would effectively represent a constant element of Postman's future research within the media pedagogy. His other early works, half a dozen books published between 1963 and 1966, are devoted to linguistics and education, the relationships between language and learning processes, and the use of language in teaching and research (Strate, 1994; Gencarelli, 2000).

Postman explored these issues by explicitly relying on the theoretical and methodological support provided by the field of study called linguistic relativity (§ 4.3), and in particular on the now well-known hypothesis based on the studies of Edward Sapir (1921) and Benjamin Whorf (1956)—one of the postulates that would subsequently become part of intellectual tradition of media ecology—that suggests language is the crucial element that guides and directs the development of cognitive processes rather than a mere expressive vessel of human thought (Postman and Weingartner, 1966; Lyons, 1981). In brief, the Sapir-Whorf hypothesis argues that language influences thought and organizes our perception of reality. Rather than merely representing the world, language creates it. In the same way, the dynamics of learning also seem to be closely connected to the expressive forms of language (Gannaway, 1994; Strate, 2003; Nystrom, 2006).

This approach emerges as the central motif of all the books Postman co-authored with his colleague from New York, Charles Weingartner; among which *Teaching as a Subversive Activity* (1969) stands out for its brilliant arguments and instant popularity. The book immediately generated a remarkable response in the movement of reform of the American educational system in the early 1970s (Strate, 2006, p. 52), and is still considered a key work in the specialized literature. Postman and Weingartner explore the role that teaching and the educational system should have in a contemporary social context dominated by the mass media's standardizing action. In their view—clearly influenced by McLuhan's pedagogical approach (Strate, 2003, p. 341; Gencarelli, 2006, p. 211)—education should play a "subversive" role or help to develop an awareness and understanding of the linguistic mechanisms conveyed by media that invisibly shape human behaviour.

As a medium, language itself is a cognitive environment that embraces the educational processes, and as such it should be understood, studied, and problematized. School and education should therefore promote a critical awareness, not just of the messages the media convey but of the context within which those messages are received and of the way such context influences how human experience is shaped. In other words, all media, as linguistic forms, organize the perception of reality. Aside from their content, as the authors write, «that is not that the content alone of these [new media] need be studied, but rather that the perceptual-cognitive effects on us of the form of these new languages be understood.» (Postman and Weingartner, 1969, p. 187). Such a process of awareness is the condition for a new educational environment, a «counter-argument» (p. 21), a new perceptual context within which prevailing linguistic standardization may be subverted and new communication dynamics may emerge.

In the pedagogical model proposed by Postman and Weingartner, the knowledge of prevailing linguistic forms and the development and experimentation of new linguistic forms are the elements that may generate a new kind of flexible, creative, and innovative thought and new critical, inclusive, and proactive ways of learning that may become actual "survival strategies" (p. 174) in the educational environment.

The thermostatic function of education

At the same time as *Teaching as a Subversive Activity* (1969) appeared, Postman was working to create a full academic program around media ecology at New York University as a practical and operational instrument to support his pedagogical model. Postman had illustrated some of the underlying principles of the new academic course in his speech before the annual meeting of the National Council of Teachers of English in 1968. His paper was later published under the title *The Reformed English Curriculum* (Postman, 1970), and was included two years later in *The Soft Revolution*, a book co-authored with Weingartner (Postman and Weingartner, 1971) and explicitly aimed at a potential readership of students. Besides defining the new discipline as «the study of how media of communication affect human perception, understanding, feeling, and value» (p. 139), the two authors establish four areas of research—Media History, Media Literacy and Creativity, Media Research, and Media Perspectives and Criticism (p. 140; Gencarelli, 2006, p. 214)—in order to define its peculiar features. These four areas would become the key pillars of the "soft revolution" launched within the academic and intellectual project of media ecology, therefore aimed at studying media as environments where human experience is shaped.

The Media Ecology program—which initially included doctoral programs, seminars, and meetings—was created within the New York University's Department of Culture and Communication in the early 1970s. The first doctoral dissertation (Nystrom, 1973) that organically illustrated the interpretative frame of the new field of study soon followed. Postman, however, would need a few more years to work out a sufficiently complete analysis of the postulates, method, and approach for media ecology, as well as a proposal for its operational application. The result of this phase was *Teaching as a Conserving Activity* (1979) (published in the late 1970s by Postman alone, without Weingartner's co-authorship): a brilliant theorization of the new interpretative paradigm of media in relation with the development of human educational and cultural processes. The complexity of the arguments developed in this text are such that it may be considered as the highest point of Postman's intellectual research in the field of media ecology (Gencarelli, 2006, p. 248). Since the very beginning, Postman declares a clear change of course from the arguments developed ten years previously with Weingartner. The "subversive" role then attributed to the educational and learning processes is replaced by a different but complementary vision based on a dialectic logic.

In *Teaching as a Conserving Activity* (1979), Postman argues for a new role of education and to the entirety of pedagogical processes in the contemporary society that translates into an actual activity of conservation. This is, in other words, what the author defines as the "thermostatic function" of education and school (p. 18). The recourse to such a metaphor is justified by the idea of balance and in particular by the principle of homeostasis, a quite important term borrowed from biology, that explains how living organisms react to the variation of external conditions all while keeping some inherent functions quite stable. This principle can be easily adapted to the concept of environment towards which the idea of balance plays an essential role, whether the concerned environment is natural, social, or technological.

From Postman's ecological perspective, the human environment is considered a combination of these three environments—natural, social, and technological—*vis a vis* culture. Postman reached this conclusion after reading an array of thinkers connected with the paradigm of cybernetics, and in particular with the American mathematician Norbert Wiener and the insights he proposed in his famous *The Human Use of Human Beings* (1950). Postman uses Wiener's words to introduce the principle of the thermostat in his pedagogical model—«the clearest example of cybernetics in action» (Postman, 1979, p. 21)—in order to metaphorically illustrate the function performed by the teaching processes and how they balance and rebalance the human cultural environment. In this way, the antinomy subversion/conservation—the poles of Postman's pedagogical vision—is effectively overcome. In his view, the thermostatic function of teaching is performed by «conserving tradition when the rest of the environment is innovative; or [being] innovative when the rest of the society is tradition-bound» (Postman, 1979, p. 21). In other words, any educational process results from a dialectical relation between human beings and the environment, between the development of human cognitive models and expressive forms. Therefore, the thermostatic activity of education has no goal in itself; instead it is rather an ongoing process of dynamic development whereby homeostasis is achieved in our human environment by balancing opposing cultural trends. As Postman explains, this is «an ecological rather than teleological view» (p. 22). Against the fast and frantic process of social change, the educational system has the pedagogical duty to re-establish a balance and counterbalance the prevailing trends and flows through its action of critical awareness. Postman relies on the so-called counter-cyclical theory of David Riesman, an American sociologist and pedagogist who was close to the Chicago School (§ 4.1) and well-known for his studies on human trends conceived as social phenomena (Riesman, 1950). Postman writes in this respect: «Where a culture is stressing conformity, education should stress individuality» (Postman, 1979, p. 24). And the same principle may be applied to other cultural trends based on the same homeostatic vision that should guide the educational processes conceived within a systemic and ecologic logic aimed at balancing the development dynamics of human culture that constantly move between innovation and conservation.

Given its peculiar thermostatic action, education must necessarily consider the role played by communication forms in the development of cognitive and cultural processes. Any communication form as well as any medium develops a context, a cognitive habitat—it defines an environment that influences the way of thinking and living of the individuals who live in it. For this reason, only the awareness of the nature and meaning of that environment may promote the thermostatic function performed by education and school. It is a sort of media literacy that should be developed in a pedagogical sense within the educational system. «Education», Postman writes, «conceived as a thermostatic activity, should inevitably have among its main goals helping students to rise beyond and above their own information environment, so that they may be aware of their own position» (p. 153). In a similar way, the same context of school and education may also be considered as a medium, or an educational environment, a "curriculum" (p. 35) that impacts on the organization and development of society. In other words, and this is what Postman's hypothesis suggests, educational systems should consider media as a priority concern given the role they play in shaping human experience. On the other side, the educational system should be considered as an environment, or a medium that can organize the perception of reality and promote new models of thought. In brief, the pedagogical patterns proposed by Postman in order to practically stimulate a process of critical awareness towards media environments and their influences over the development of human experience are actually the foundations of the entire tradition of media ecology studies. From this point of view—and this is the main element Postman contributed to this study field—his intellectual proposition is media education, thus educating *to* media, which also includes recognizing the pedagogical function the media environment has. The general goal of media ecology is therefore «observing culture as a system of media forms that reflect and at the same time create the prevailing vision» (p. 164). It is with this awareness that media ecology places at the core of its operational survey a fully complementary relationship between observer and observed, human and environment, human thought and its expressive forms, considered in their simultaneous presence within the same cultural habitat.

How to survive the technopoly

The works published by Postman starting in the early 1980s show a clear change of approach towards the dynamics of the development of media in his contemporary culture. Indeed, in the scholar's estimation, the thermostatic equilibrium of then-contemporary culture was dramatically compromised—as Postman clearly argues—by the impact of a mass medium like television. In *The Disappearance of Childhood* (1982), Postman uncompromisingly exposes the negative role of television. In his view, the existential condition of childhood is clearly damaged by the new media environment shaped by TV's pervasive presence. The overload of information and cognitive stimuli one is subjected to in childhood is such that its experiential and learning processes slowly and gradually dissolve into adulthood. *Amusing Ourselves to Death* (1985), probably one of Postman's best-known books, is an even more radical criticism of TV and the cultural industry's impact on education and learning processes. In a society that is unwittingly subjected to the *diktat* of the media and entertainment function—the text mirrors the postmodern ideas of Debord, Orwell, Huxley (Strate, 1994; 2014)—critical conscience succumbs to the invisible pressure and insidious addiction of show-business, with an inevitable impact on educational and learning processes that would be analyzed in a further book, *The End of Education* (1995).

With *Technopoly* (1992), Postman goes back to his meditations on media and industrial culture and extends his focus to technology and its relationships with forms of power and knowledge. He sees the uncontrolled progress of technological development as the reflection of a modern kind of monopoly, namely a "technopoly" (the last in the three phases he recognizes in the history of technology within human culture (p. 27)) to which contemporary individuals are unwittingly subjected: «One characteristic of those who live in a Technopoly is that they are largely unaware of both the origins and the effects of their technologies» (p. 128). The text is a radical exposé that transversally involves several social and cultural fields, from economics to politics, from information to social sciences, from medical practices to so-called scientism (p. 133), all equally influenced by a sort of technological rule that, while in many ways invisible, effectively exists as a technocratic totalitarianism brilliantly and wittily exposed by Postman. That said, Postman's argument is neither a mere unmerciful criticism of technological progress, nor an "apocalyptic" statement against the contemporary society. Precisely because he is aware of the delicate balance that rules the forms of human culture considered in their environmental dimension, and is the foundation of media ecology, Postman's approach is aimed once more at recognizing education as a key process that can influence the environmental powers that impact on the balance of human society and culture. Postman's ecological approach therefore insists on the emancipation processes that are deeply rooted in the humanistic tradition and argues for the need for a subject to become a critical inhabitant and citizen who is aware of all the environments he belongs to. The revival of a new Enlightenment-influenced humanism will indeed be the subject of his following book, *Building a Bridge to the 18th Century* (Postman, 1999). During the same years, at the opening of the Media Ecology Association's first annual meeting, Postman reaffirmed the humanistic element in media ecology by explaining that, if «a medium may be defined as an environment within which a culture grows» (2000, p. 20): the human being has the ability to counterbalance the powers that emerge within the same environment.

From a humanistic point of view, this means considering media as primary forms of existence, that in Postman's pedagogical thought become invisible processes that can be used to rediscover the deepest roots of the complex system of values and knowledge that underlie the entire human ecology.

Neil Postman's main works
Television and the Teaching of English (1961)
Linguistics. A Revolution in Teaching (1966), with Weingartner C.
Teaching as a Subversive Activity (1969), with Weingartner C.
The Soft Revolution (1971), with Weingartner C.
Teaching as a Conserving Activity (1979)
The Disappearance of Childhood (1982)
Amusing Ourselves to Death (1985)
Technopoly (1992)
The End of Education (1995)
Building a Bridge to the 18th Century (1999)

Further readings
Gencarelli T.F. (2000), "The Intellectual Roots of Media Ecology in the Thought and Work of Neil Postman", *The New Jersey Journal of Communication*, 8, 1, pp. 91-103.
Gencarelli T.F. (2006), "Neil Postman and the Rise of Media Ecology", in Lum C.M.K., ed, *Perspectives in Culture, Technology and Communication*, Hampton Press, Cresskill, NJ, pp. 201-253.
Rose P. (2016), *Confronting Technopoly*, Intellect, Bristol (UK).
Strate L. (1994), "Post(modern)man, or Neil Postman as a Postmodernist", *Etc. A Review of General Semantics*, 51, 2, pp. 159-170.
Strate L. (2003), "Neil Postman, Defender of the Word", *Etc. A Review of General Semantics*, 60, 4, pp. 341-350.
Strate L. (2014), *Amazing ourselves to death. Neil Postman's brave new world revisited*, Peter Lang, New York.

3. The Toronto School

Between the 1930s and 1970s, a remarkable intellectual climate coalesced within and around the University of Toronto. During this time, intellectual giants such as Harold Innis, Eric Havelock, Northrop Frye, and Marshall McLuhan, among others, captured the global imagination. This scholarly community came to be known as The Toronto School of Communication Theory (Watson and Blondheim, 2007), achieving international recognition for its innovative and trans-disciplinary approaches to emerging social and cultural challenges. This school of thought gave voice to a transforming vision of perception and social order brought about by the evolving possibilities of interconnectivity enmeshed in developing media technologies and creative energy.

Deeply interdisciplinary, the Toronto school constitutes an "invisible college" (Griffith and Mullins 1972), a school of thought sharing «a set of similar theoretical underpinnings, perspectives, or questions for understanding culture, technology, and communication» (Crane 1972, 128) which have gone beyond academia to have a lasting impact in art and culture. The influence of the Toronto School was in fact exerted not only upon subsequent scholars, but also upon culture more broadly through the literature of Margaret Atwood, a former student of both McLuhan and Frye; the visual art of Harley Parker, Sheila and Wilfred Watson, Sorel Etrog; and the music of Glenn Gould, whose McLuhan-inspired collected writings and extensive discography constitute relics of a unique, Toronto-inspired intellectual milieu.

Attempts to define the significance of the Toronto School in a manner rivalling that of the Frankfurt or Chicago schools have been attempted and strive to «acknowledge once again that we are inheritors of Innis's and McLuhan's views of communication» (Hanke

2008, p. 268). Scholars continue to explore the impact of McLuhan and Innis on our understanding of the mediated world around us, to codify what constitutes a Canadian or Toronto-specific school of thought (Kroker 1986; Babe 2000), and to extend the preoccupations of the founding thinkers of the Toronto School to nearly all facets of art, literature, and culture (Lamberti 2012, Powe 2014). In fact, whether a Toronto School actually exists or not has been forever a point of contention within North American media studies—and, the discussion is far from over given the lack of unanimity in this regard. Some supported its existence in various ways (de Kerckhove 1989), some reacted with a certain skepticism (Carpenter 1992), while others produced a detailed account (Theall 1986) of an intellectual endeavor that, beyond any assessment of method, remains undoubtedly relevant particularly in terms of its contribution to media ecology as field of study. The heated discussions that particularly raged through the sphere of McLuhan studies have been described at length elsewhere (Lamberti, 2000, p. 171; Watson and Blondheim, 2007, p. 21).

What is certain is that, from the 1930s to the 1970s, Toronto was an undoubtedly relevant intellectual centre that witnessed the emergence of a number of scholars whose shared intellectual interests were instrumental in drawing worldwide attention to the provocative idea that technological engagement plays a fundamental role in the structuring of human perception and culture. The very development of communication and media studies as an academic discipline owes much to the formative Toronto School scholars. Toronto and its university offered the best breeding ground for multi-faceted and diversified thought that easily embraced thinkers from across Canada and abroad, who successfully worked in the same place and at the same time, therefore sharing the same cultural *milieu* and, sometimes, even the same views, although articulated in different ways. Therefore, while it might not fit into the orthodox description of a school of thought—although described in the 1980s as a canonized 'school' of thought (Berg, 1985; Theall 1986; Kerckhove 1989)—that is the origin of what is now informally described as the Toronto School.

The following pages are devoted to the main protagonists of this intellectual venture, starting with the political economist

Harold Innis (§ 3.1), who, in spite of the pressing courtship from the Chicago academic context where he had spent a fruitful portion of his career, accepted a teaching post at the University of Toronto in 1939. He would be joined there by Marshall McLuhan (§ 3.2) only nine years later, in 1946. Along with the anthropologist Ted Carpenter, who in the meantime had relocated to Toronto from the US, McLuhan founded a journal, *Explorations*, and initiated a varied and quite vibrant research project. During the same years, precisely from 1929 to 1947, the University of Toronto also attracted Eric Havelock. A classicist of British origins who admired Innis (Havelock, 1982; Gronbeck), Havelock played a key role, along with McLuhan and Milman Parry, in the intellectual development of another prominent representative of the School, Walter Ong (§ 3.3), who, while teaching at Saint Louis in the US, effectively cooperated with the School by contributing an organic and systematic frame to its often fragmentary approach. Along with these pioneers, other relevant figures should be remembered for their work in Toronto's intellectual environment of the time. Northrop Frye in particular stands out as the literary theorist and critic whose rivalry with McLuhan would generate a gossipy kind of interest around the School's affairs. What is indisputable is that, although with some distinctions, Frye and McLuhan worked in the same intellectual area and should be seen as equals (Guardiani, 1991, 1996; Watson and Blondheim 2007; Powe, 2014), having shared the same creative approach which has gone beyond academia to have a lasting impact in art and culture.

This group of scholars often had opportunities to attend discussion meetings (Buxton, 2004) and to gather in informal settings. Some observers of the time report that the Royal Ontario Museum's coffee shop, within walking distance from the University of Toronto campus, was for a short period the daily theatre of heated debates and long conversations (Theall, 1986; Morrison, 2006, p. 166). Besides Carpenter, McLuhan, and Frye, these meetings were occasionally attended by Innis himself, by the Greek anthropologist Dorothy Lee, the Swiss architectural historian Sigfried Giedion, the anthropologist and psychologist Ray Birdwhistell, the Austrian economist Peter Drucker, and the visionary genius Buckminster Fuller.

When, in 1953, a substantial research grant gave Carpenter and McLuhan the opportunity to initiate the editorial activity of the *Explorations* group—the vibrant core of a fruitful cross-disciplinary research until 1959 (Carpenter, 1992)—the journal attracted a wide range of personalities, variously related to Toronto's intellectual scene, including the economist Tom Easterbrook, Jacqueline Tyrwhitt (an urban planner who had studied with Patrick Geddes), and the psychologist Carl Williams. Over the years, these would be joined by many others who sought the opportunity to develop their approach in a vibrant and stimulating environment such as the Centre for Culture and Technology directed by McLuhan. This second group included Harley Parker and Wilfred Watson, who co-authored two collections of writings with McLuhan; as well as a host of valuable essayists, including Berrington Nevitt (1982), Donald Theall (2001), Frank Zingrone (2001), Eric McLuhan (2011), David Olson (1979), Bob Logan (2004, 2013), Derrick De Kerckhove (1990, 1991, 1995). Each gave a relevant contribution to the body of ideas and research constituting a key studies in media ecology.

3.1 Harold Innis and the ecology of knowledge

If there is a thinker that should be credited for pioneering the intellectual tradition currently known as media ecology within Canadian academia, it is Harold A. Innis (1894-1952). A brilliant economist, an expert on Canadian models of industrial and commercial development, a historian of communication, a theorist of human culture and its social and political structures, Innis left a legacy that is certainly one of the essential benchmarks in late twentieth-century socio-economical studies. The new paradigm his work opened for the North American intellectual environment would effectively guide an entire generation of later media and communication researchers—from Marshall McLuhan (§ 3.2) to Neil Postman (§ 2.3), among the others (Melody et al., 1981).

Born in Otterville, a small village in south-western Ontario, Innis spent his childhood in the country, well aware of the difficulties of farming, an experience that would mark him indelibly.

Being uncommonly thirsty for knowledge, Innis decided to study law, politics and economics at McMaster University, a stimulating Baptist-run college then located in nearby Toronto (Watson, 2006, p. 64). As a country boy, although transplanted in the city, Innis witnessed the development of the major early twentieth-century inventions that would later become the object of his studies: the transformation of hunting and fishing into the production of basic commodities, the development of the railway network, the birth and development of the radio. At the same time, he was a first-hand witness of the Great War's horrors, as he served in northern France on the bloody frontline of Vimy Ridge (Creighton, 1957, p. 34). Having received a leg wound in the war, he was returned home where he chose the title *The Returned Soldier* for his M.A. thesis, a review of the devastating social effects of war on a generation of young Canadians who, just like him, had directly or indirectly experienced the cruelty of war.

Once he completed his studies at McMaster University, Innis' interests shifted from law and politics to economics. In this sense, his subsequent experience at the University of Chicago would be as fundamental as the intellectual influence of the economist Thorstein Veblen (Czitrom, 1982, pp. 149-151; Carey, 1989, p. 103; Stamps, 1995, pp. 55-56) and of the founders of the Chicago School of Urban Sociology—Robert Park, Ernest Burgess, Roderick McKenzie (§ 4.1): at the time, the cradle of sociological research engaged in North American pragmatist approaches. Particularly inspired by Veblen's unconventional approach, although he never had a chance to meet him in person, Innis obtained his PhD under the guide of the historian of economics Chester Wright with a dissertation on the history of the Canadian Pacific Railway, then the largest railway network in Canada. This and a host of later works about the fur trade, cod fishery, and gold mining quickly earned Innis a certain clout with the regional government commissions and Canadian economic institutions with which he began to cooperate thereby earning a certain influence over the next few years. His studies actually provided the foundation for an approach oriented towards the understanding of Canada's economic history that would conflate wide-ranging and heterogeneous visions, from the analysis of commercial flows to telecommunication infrastructure (Patterson, 1990). Such approach underlies Innis' research on the means of production, preservation and dissemination of knowledge that would almost entirely absorb his later intellectual efforts (Drache, 1995; Acland, Buxton, 2000). The Chicago academic milieu, where he had actually become a well-established expert, would try to lure him there, but in 1937 he was appointed full political economy professor at the University of Toronto where he would remain until 1952, the year of his premature death following an incurable illness.

Aside from the substantial body of preparatory studies made of articles, reports, and economic analyses of various nature developed during the US phase (Christian, 1980), the main core of Innis' theoretical production includes three books, all published between 1950 and 1952. In the last of these published posthumously just a few months after his death—*Changing Concepts of Time* (1952)—Innis developed the arguments presented in the first two books and tried to apply them to contemporary reality by offering a radical approach—in some ways similar to the positions of the Frankfurt School theorists (Stamps, 1995)—that implicitly but clearly criticized the economic, social, and cultural policies then-prevalent in the US. The influence of American advertising, mass media, and cultural industry was such—the author argues—that it generated a hegemonical and inhibitory effect over the economical development in Canada (Czitrom, 1982; Heyer, 2006). If one excludes this last work, Innis' contribution can be fully understood by studying *Empire and Communications* (1950) and *The Bias of Communication* (1951), two "classics" that left a lasting mark on what would be later known as the Toronto School of Communication (Watson, Blondheim, 2007).

Communication and its empires

The research Innis conducted since the 1930s on the economic control over raw materials and so-called staples—basic commodities that can actually influence the development dynamics of a society—led him to extend his interest beyond the mere means of production of primary goods to the control of the immaterial forms of knowledge, as well as on the physical supports through which these are produced, preserved and propagated. In other words, he understood the value of communication as a material good, a basic commodity or a raw material that should be preserved, and the control of which is closely related to the economic and political development of a society. Innis believes that the forms of production, preservation, and propagation of knowledge underlie the development of any civilization or society in any historical age. The concept of monopoly of basic commodities is therefore extended to the forms of communication and the realm of knowledge. In this regard, Innis introduced the concept of "monopoly of knowledge" (Innis, 1950, p. 71) to precisely describe the control of the forms of development, preservation, and sharing of knowledge. This means that, in any empire, society or state, the ascent, stabilization, and sharing of power depends on the ability to manage the different forms of communication, as well as on the choice of the material media through which these are channeled in space and time. Indeed, Innis argues that the forms of communication may be oriented in order to exert the monopoly of knowledge across time or space. The longevity of the medium or, conversely, the ease of transportation impact the possibilities of consolidating such monopoly. In other words, Innis argues that the fate of a civilization depends on the balance created in the management of power between the two dimensions of space and time. The dimension of time is related to heavy, hardly movable media, such as writing on stone, which are more enduring for this reason. The dimension of space rather belongs to light media that can be easily moved but are more liable to decay into oblivion. The forms of knowledge that can withstand the wear and tear of time promote the decentralization and expansion of power, while those that can be easily transported and distributed across space promote centralization, consolidation, and the preservation of power.

Innis reaches these insights through the development of a wide-ranging and well-documented *History of Communications*, a book that would never entirely see the light (Peters et al., 2014), although its arguments would appear in two important works that together represent a gigantic challenge to the conventions of knowledge. In particular, *Empire and Communications* (1950), a more or less organic collection of insights compiled for a cycle of lectures held at Oxford, describes a history of the forms of communication and of the control of knowledge by controlling interests—usually emperors, kings, or priestly castes—that since the oldest civilizations in the Western world exerted or tried to exert a monopoly of knowledge so powerful that it could more or less significantly impact on the development of empires, dynasties, and societies. His approach expresses a philosophy of history and an organic and unitary view of human development that effectively denies the myth of boundless progress, an evolutionary, linear, and deterministic process resulting from the Enlightenment and a historicist model of the modern age. In other words, Innis broke free from the ideology of progress in order to consider the ways through which societies find their inner balance in time and space. Therefore, the development of human history is nothing but the succession of different forms of production, preservation, and propagation of knowledge that, time after time and based on a cyclical and differential logic, naturally result from social development.

In *Empire and Communications*, Innis discusses a long series of political, religious, and bureaucratic events in the human civilization: from the clash between monarchical power and priestly castes in ancient Egypt to the control of the first forms of phonetic transcription that contributed to the empire's organization in Babylon; from the sacred character of writing in the Jewish culture to the interweaving of oral and written culture in ancient Greece; from the written text as a form of affirmation of power in imperial Rome to the parchment codes of Christian culture in the Byzantine Empire; from the ecclesiastical control over paper in the Middle Ages to the propagation of movable type print in the modern age, down to the most recent forms of monopoly of power connected to the emergence of nationalism and colonial imperialism, and to the hegemony exerted through the power of newspapers and the political use of the new radio medium. As Innis argued: «Monopolies of knowledge had developed and declined partly in relation to the medium of communication on which they were built and tended to alternate as they emphasized religion, decentralization, and space» (Innis, 1950, p. 253). The communication media, or the system of the expressive forms of power and knowledge are therefore conceived within Innis' theoretical framework as peculiar functions of the dominant groups of power within a larger social, dynamic, and constantly rebalancing process that determines the birth, consolidation or decline of civilizations. Therefore, due to a circular and differential process, the communication forms used by a society and its hegemonic groups in order to exert a monopolistic power actually work retroactively on the attitudes, habits, and decisions of the same society that created them.

The Bias of Communication

The Bias of Communication (1951) is a rather less organic and more fragmented collection; a sprawling mosaic of seemingly heterogeneous and obscure insights that result in a far from accessible text. With all its non-linearity, and the combination of arguments it contains, the book reflects an approach that aims at finding a connection between phenomena that are apparently unrelated in time and space. Innis merely explains his vision of the dynamic of change, of the recurrent pattern shared by elements that would be apparently so different from each other, so that it is the reader who should find a logical order in this mosaic. The book starts with a foreword, almost a provocation proposed by Innis starting from the teaching of James Ten Broeke, his professor at McMaster University, articulated as follows: «Why do we attend to the things to which we attend?» (Innis, 1951, p. 23). This question, almost a tautology, is nothing but a trick to directly introduce the main issue of the work, or the focus on the influence exerted by communication forms on the processes that govern the development of knowledge. Innis believes that the communication media literally shape a vision of the world, the social issues that inform a certain age, by facilitating the emergence of new cultural paradigms that in turn will shape new expressive means, new forms of knowledge, based on a circular logic of mutual reciprocity. Therefore, Innis tries to demonstrate that «the use of a medium of communication over a long period will to some extent determine the character of knowledge to be communicated» (p. 55).

In other words, he insists on the fact that the communication forms acquired in a certain society impact on the choice of "the things to which we attend". But at the same time, he warns, «the changes of "the things to which we attend" will be followed by changes in communication» (p. 23), or new transformations in the realm of the communication processes. In brief, the things *through which* we think influence the *very things* we think about.

Innis' insistence on the prominent role the forms of communication and their inherent material and technological nature have for the understanding of a certain age or society, or for the definition of the factors of change in large historical processes, made him the target of a remarkable amount of criticism: the most recurring accusation being an exaggerated deterministic approach, a sort of reductionism to the mere material and technological aspects viewed as the agents that define social development (Smith and Marx, 1994). The accusation of technological determinism is frequently invoked in many assessments of Innis' approach in North American academic contexts (Carey, 1967), and also accepted in the European circles (Flichy, 1995). Although Innis would be considered a noble and academic father with a consistent curriculum in the genealogy of media and communication studies, as well as an undisputed pioneer (Havelock, 1982), this is an accusation that would somehow always follow him. In recent years, many experts have tried to refute the accusation levelled against him (Heyer, 2006) by rightly arguing for the existence of a circularity in the relationship between society and technology that perhaps can only be inferred from his approach. In fact, Innis' meditations provide a quite convincing explanation for the phase during which, once technology is stabilized in a society by the dominant groups, its presence acts deeply and influences the processes of social change. In other words, Innis' determinism implies a partial rather than an erroneous view of technologies in that it only considers their impact on society. This said, there is still the challenge of considering the relevance of such impact within a larger process that is at the same time technological and social (Murphie and Potts, 2003).

The argument at the core of *The Bias of Communication* (1951) is represented by the word *bias*, a term that has wide-ranging and somewhat ambiguous semantic implications. However, there are two meanings that are commonly combined with its use within Innis' theoretical approach. On one side, *bias* is used as a synonym of influence, mechanism of control, conditioning, or more simply it expresses a tendency. Therefore, every society tends to be characterized by a dominant factor, function, or medium that can exert a certain influence on the economical, political, and cultural development of that society across space and time. This occurs through a process of conditioning or, in a more evident form, of control of the means of production, preservation, and propagation of knowledge. In other terms, every age or human society has its own *bias*; that is, there is one communication form that more than others tends to exert a function of influence, control, and conditioning over the social development of that same age or society. One of the purposes of media theory is therefore the understanding of that tendency. On the other side, the semantic implication of *bias* indicates a disposition, a constraint, a structure, or literally a distortion or cultural preconception. This means recognizing that the influence, control, or conditioning exerted by a communication form occurs within a range of boundaries and possibilities that are inherent to that same communication form. In other words, the fundamental bias is inherent to that medium's fundamental structure and is precisely a structural constraint, an element that is inherently socially determined as well as determining. The task of media theory is therefore understanding the fundamental disposition, the deep bias that is inherent to every medium. In brief, we may say that in trying to understand that inherent nature of a communication medium, the concept of bias, meant as a disposition/prejudice or influence/tendency, is intended to understand respectively its *structure* and its *action*.

The realms of knowledge

There is actually a third interpretative option that, once and for all, relates Innis to the intellectual tradition of media ecology and even legitimizes his role as an undisputed pioneer within Canadian academia and culture. First of all, *bias* is a concept of a monopoly of knowledge—a definition that, as we have seen, he introduced in *Empire and communications* (1950). Therefore, considered in light of the circular relationship between technology and society, between expressive forms and social issues, between material and cultural factors, this term should be viewed, within Innis' theoretical system, in its metaphorical meaning as the clarification of the complex and dynamic balance—another keyword in Innis' philosophy (Eyer, 2006, p. 153)—that regulates the relationships between media and human culture. Therefore, *bias* should be seen first of all as the expression of equilibrium in the social processes that as such are defined by, and at the same time define, forms of knowledge. Far from being linear or deterministic, the dynamics of social processes acquire a systemic configuration. *Bias* is therefore the system of factors within which human culture grows and develops, a long-range systemic process that shapes a civilization. *Bias* is actually the shape acquired by social and technological structures in a certain historical age. In other words, given the symbiotic relationship that, according to Innis, connects human beings and technology (Carey, 1967, p. 7), *bias* is most simply the media environment within which people happen to live. In brief, Innis' concept of bias expresses an actual ecology of knowledge. Actually, this interpretation can be seen to reflect the ecological approach to social organization proposed by Robert Park (1952), a key member of the Chicago School (§ 4.1) who influenced Innis' research. Therefore, the concept of social ecology represents the main insight that would lead Innis to opt for an idea of media as actual technological, cultural, and communication environments rather than mere instruments or channels for the social transmission of knowledge. This remarkably important conceptual leap legitimizes Innis as the link that connects the US and Canadian intellectual traditions: «the most eminent member of the Chicago group headed by Robert Park» (McLuhan, 1964b, p. 22). Innis may be considered as the pioneer of an ecological approach to knowledge, the forerunner of an environmental vision of communication forms, «the first one to see in the media our most important environment, although barely perceptible» (Kuhns, 1972, p. 168). Therefore, the medium is a communication environment, a technological habitat (Kroker,

1984, p. 107) that provides the breeding ground of habits, needs and tendencies of human culture, in particular those related to the production, preservation, and propagation of knowledge. Media are thus conceived as «infrastructures of being, the habitats and materials through which we act and are. This gives them ecological, ethical, and existential import» (Peters, 2015, p. 15). The entire history of human civilization develops around the control of such forms and is marked by monopolies of power that are never stable precisely because the pulsating rhythm of the human environment is unstable, dynamic, and complex.

Harold Innis's main works
A History of the Canadian Pacific Railway (1923)
The Fur Trade in Canada (1930)
The Cod Fisheries (1940)
Empire and Communications (1950)
The Bias of Communication (1951)
Changing Concepts of Time (1952)

Further readings
Bonnett J. (2013) *Emergence and empire. Innis, complexity, and the trajectory of history*, McGill-Queen's University Press, Montreal.
Buxton W.J., Acland C.R., eds. (1999), *Harold Innis in the new century. Reflections and refractions*, McGill-Queen's University Press, Montreal.
Buxton W.J. (2002), "The Rise of McLuhanism, The Loss of Innis-sense: Rethinking the Origins of the Toronto School of Communication", *Canadian Journal of Communication*, 37, pp. 577-593.
Buxton W.J., ed. (2013), *Harold Innis and the North*, McGill-Queen's University Press, Montreal.
Buxton W.J., Cheney M.R., Heyer P., eds (2015), *Harold Innis's History of communications. Paper and printing. Antiquity to early modernity*, Rowman & Littlefield, Lanham, Maryland.
Buxton W.J., Cheney M.R., Heyer P., eds (2016), *Harold Innis reflects. Memoir and WWI writings/correspondence*, Rowman & Littlefield, Lanham, Maryland.
Carey J.W. (1967), "Harold Innis and Marshall McLuhan", *Antioch Review*, 27, 1, pp. 5-39.
Christian W. (1980), *The Idea Files of Harold Adams Innis*, University of Toronto Press, Toronto.
Creighton D.G. (1957), *Harold Adams Innis. Portrait of a Scholar*, University of Toronto Press, Toronto.

Drache D., ed. (1995), *Staples, Markets, and Cultural change. Selected essays by Harold Innis*, McGill-Queen's University Press, Montreal.
Heyer P. (2003), *Harold Innis*, Rowman & Littlefield, Boulder.
Heyer P. (2006), "Harold Innis' Legacy in the Media Ecology Tradition", in Lum C.M.K., ed., *Perspectives on Culture, Technology and Communication: The Media Ecology Tradition*, Hampton Press, Cresskill, NJ, pp. 143-161.
Kroker A. (1984), *Technology and the Canadian Mind: Innis/ McLuhan/ Grant*, New World Perspectives, Montreal.
Melody W.H., Salter L., Heyer P., eds. (1981), *Culture, Communication and Dependency. The Tradition of H.A. Innis*, Ablex, Norwood.
Patterson G. (1990), *History and Communications: Harold Innis, Marshall McLuhan, the Interpretation of History*, University of Toronto Press, Toronto.
Neill R. (1972), *A New Theory of Value: The Canadian Economics of H.A. Innis*, University of Toronto Press, Toronto.
Stamps J. (1995), *Unthinking Modernity: Innis, McLuhan and the Frankfurt School*, McGill-Queen's University Press, Montreal.
Watson A.J. (2006), *Marginal Man. The Dark Vision of Harold Innis*, University of Toronto Press, Toronto.

3.2 Marshall McLuhan and the Aesthetics of Media

No author in the field of media and communication studies has been more quoted, analyzed, and sometimes even misunderstood than Herbert Marshall McLuhan (1911-1980). He was certainly an unusual and provocative thinker, and his profile as an unconventional, anti-academic scholar who tried to overcome the traditional practices of humanistic research has generated extensive debates regarding his method, insights, and catchphrases, often compounded by critical analysis of the very validity of his statements. Most important, however, is the impact McLuhan's ideas have had on the study of humanities more broadly. As a result, scholars of media and communication have reacted by choosing one of two separate approaches. On one side, over the fifty years since its appearance, the reception of McLuhan's thought seems to have congealed into a normalized, tepid, *à la page*, "vernacular Mcluhanism" (Ortoleva, 2011) aligned with the host of other media theories produced across the twentieth century, and faithfully illustrated by any specialized textbook. This version of

McLuhan's thought preserves and presents the original tenets of McLuhan's thought as well as the well-known aphorisms— from "the medium is the message" to the "global village"—to a wide and transversal audience, thereby effectively overcoming the closed boundaries of various academic fields. On the other side, the heritage of McLuhan's thought has continued to stimulate and fascinate a specific group of scholars who were rather interested in approaching the study of media not necessarily from a specialized perspective, usually based in a specific disciplinary field— very often sociology, perhaps the only discipline that McLuhan never practiced—because they saw the study of media as a tool that could be used to approach other disciplinary fields, or at least to establish a dialogue with them. In other words, whatever the place it took among the theories of media and communication, and beyond the oracular power that attracted the attention of many observers, McLuhan's thought seems to have achieved its best results outside the closed circle of media studies. All the while remaining rooted in the humanities, McLuhan's thought effectively attracted the interest of scholars from other disciplinary fields who were particularly interested in a transversal or truly cross-disciplinary approach to knowledge. This is the case of the intellectual tradition of media ecology within which McLuhan is undoubtedly considered as a primary figure whose contribution has been largely recognized, valued, and in many ways reassessed over the years (Levinson, 2000; Strate and Wachtel, 2005; Morrison, 2006; Strate, 2008; Logan, 2013).

Born in Edmonton in 1911, in 1928 he moved to Winnipeg in order to study at the local University of Manitoba. McLuhan first studied in the engineering program but in a radical change of course began studying English literature, driven by an insatiable appetite for knowledge that targeted the entire range of the humanities, from rhetoric to philosophy, from linguistics to art history (Marchand, 1989, p. 16). After graduation, he had the opportunity to travel to Cambridge, the cradle of European literary criticism, to pursue his studies. There, from 1934 to 1936, he studied in close contact with highly influential scholars such as Ivor A. Richards (1893-1979) and Frank R. Leavis (1895-1978), two of the pioneers of New Criticism, an intellectual school that at the time actually revolutionized literary criticism on both shores of the Atlantic and that would radically influence McLuhan himself and lead him to question some of the tenets of the Victorian critical canon he had studied at Manitoba in order to explore new research directions within literature as an essential interpretive key and a fundamental ground for the understanding of ongoing social and cultural changes (Lamberti, 2012, p. 140). While studying in England, he was presented with an opportunity to expand and refine his approach to literature studies by benefiting from an intellectual environment that would prove extremely stimulating for his development on an academic but as well as on a personal level. In Trinity Hall, McLuhan studied the works of the Modernists, thereby partially amending the approach of New Criticism (Willmott, 1996, p. 30). While at Cambridge, McLuhan also found out about Gilbert K. Chesterton (1874-1936) whose works would trigger a deep existential decision in the young scholar who, coming from a Protestant family, converted to Roman Catholicism in 1937 (Gordon, 1997, p. 56; Person, 2012). Such interest in the Catholic church, combined with a sincere devotion, represented more than a mere profession of faith for McLuhan ever since. As testified by a posthumous collection of writings (McLuhan, 1999), the Canadian scholar always returned to religious perspectives as the key to an organized, consistent vision at the same time rooted in a tradition of thought that would provide him with a privileged point of view for the observation of social reality: this is still a focal element of interest within the area of McLuhan studies (Pietropaolo and Logan, 2014).

After returning from England, McLuhan decided to go to the United States, first at the University of Wisconsin, and later, from 1937 to 1944, at Saint Louis University, in Missouri, where he met the Jesuit Walter Ong (§ 3.3). Ong, who was one of his students although they were the same age, became a friend with whom McLuhan would establish a stimulating and enduring intellectual relationship (Ong, 1989). At the end of this experience in the United States, McLuhan, who in the meantime had completed his PhD at Cambridge with a dissertation on the English writer Thomas Nashe and the classical pedagogy of *Trivium* (published posthumously (McLuhan, 2006)), went back to Canada to teach at

Assumption College, a Catholic University in Windsor (Marchand, 1989, p. 71). There he came in touch with Wyndham Lewis, a poet, painter, and writer of British origin, who was in town for an annual series of seminars. A co-founder of the Vorticist movement in art, Lewis was a charismatic man who would deeply influence McLuhan's intellectual development, as testified by a close correspondence between the two (Molinaro et al., 1987). On one side, these are the years when McLuhan emerged as a "man of letters" (Lamberti, 2005), a brilliant critic with a remarkable interpretive skill, an insightful commentator of a wide array of authors from Shakespeare to Blake, from Tennyson to Poe, from the Modernists Joyce, Eliot, Ford, Pound, whom he would personally be acquainted with to the Symbolists Mallarmé, Rimbaud, Baudelaire or the Romantics Coleridge and Keats (McLuhan, 1969a). On the other side, the young scholar had a precocious awareness of the deep changes that were intervening in society at the time due to an increasingly pervasive mass culture that neither avant-garde criticism and much less the then-prevailing orthodox literary canon seemed to be equipped to read and comprehend. However, it was precisely this seeming difficulty that inspired McLuhan to create a truly original way of observing society in a critical way by finding in his literary approach the fundamental basis of his approach to media, technology, and social change (Lamberti, 2000, 2005, 2012; Elder, 2013. p. 118). By combining and giving equal treatment to elitist and mass cultural forms, the expressions of so-called "high" and pop culture—an assemblage of advertisement, comics, newspaper headlines, illustrated magazines would be the object, a few years down the line, of his first book, *The Mechanical Bride* (1951)—the young literature professor would become a keen interpreter of his time, a successful reader of then-contemporary cultural, social, and environmental developments (Lamberti, 2000, p. 21); a scholar who sensed the emergence of a new postmodern paradigm and understood the need to view media as environments first and foremost capable of shaping the perceptive and cognitive structures human beings use to act on and experience the world.

In 1946, St. Michael's College, a Catholic institution within the University of Toronto, offered McLuhan employment as chair of English Literature (Gordon, 1997, p. 135). This advancement in his career marked the beginning of a fruitful period of research, in spite of the fact that the new academic environment—that also housed a renowned institute of medieval studies—was not exactly aligned with the approach of a scholar who, while an established literature professor and a practicing Catholic, was determined to turn his full attention to mass media forms. This utterly original interest, combined with the mixed reaction of his colleagues at St. Michael's led him to look for support elsewhere, both outside his own department and in other non-academic environments. This is how he established a tight collaboration, and a long friendship with the anthropologist Edmund (Ted) Carpenter, himself a professor at the University of Toronto. Their eccentric and unconventional collaboration resulted in the creation of the *Explorations* journal (McLuhan and Carpenter, 1960) funded by the Ford Foundation. During those years, McLuhan often visited New York at the invitation of Louis Forsdale, who taught at Columbia University, and attended the meetings of the National Council of Teachers of English as well as hold seminars at the Columbia University. There he met Neil Postman (§ 2.3), who was greatly interested in his areas of research and approach. The two scholars established an important intellectual collaboration (Forsdale, 1989, p. 171; Marchand, 1989, p. 132; Gordon, 1997, p. 227) aimed at propagating McLuhan's bold ideas in New York's academic and cultural environment.

In the late 1950s, Carpenter relocated from Toronto to the University of California, while the National Association of Educational Broadcasters commissioned McLuhan with a study on the educational impact of media. With *Report on Project in Understanding Media* (McLuhan, 1960), McLuhan started developing the thematic cores of his two most successful works, *The Gutenberg Galaxy* (1962), a dense *pastiche* of quotations and sometimes dazzling insights, and *Understanding Media* (1964a), a classic of McLuhan's thought and an academic success that brought him to the peak of his popularity also due to his oratorial verve, knack for witty remarks, innate passion for aphorisms, paradoxes, provocations, and puns. Partly to confine the activities of the eclectic professor, and partly to provide him with an independent workspace, in 1963 the University of Toronto granted him a modest fund to open and manage a Centre for Culture and Technology, later located in a former coach house on the St. Michael's campus. Within this modest facility, McLuhan was free to develop an intense program of seminars that attracted the interest of many students from across the campus and colleagues and scholars from a number of disciplines who wanted to study electronic media and the new, emerging area of research represented by these schoalrs (Gordon, 1997, p. 193). As an environment of interconnection, dialogue, exploration, and play, that coach house became the propelling engine of McLuhan's activities. In time, the general public became aware of him through a host of clichés—communication guru, oracle of media, and shaman of the global village—that would trap him in many ways and are still used as primary identifiers of his legacy.

Since then, as it was perhaps inevitable, McLuhan's public persona as the "High Priest of PopCult"—as he was defined in a long *Playboy* interview (McLuhan, 1969b)—was promoted through many TV appearances and by the general success of *The Medium is the Massage*, a peculiar little book assembled by graphic designer Quentin Fiore (McLuhan and Fiore, 1967). This success was followed by a period of rapid decline of popularity. The Sixties, or the decade of success, would be followed by a decade of editorial failures (Marchand, 1989, p. 212): the relative lack of success of *From Cliché to Archetype* (McLuhan and Watson, 1970), *Culture is Our Business* (1970), and *Take Today*, (McLuhan e Nevitt, 1972) and of decreasing attention from the public seemed to avenge that part of the academic community that was clearly hostile to him. Yet, at the same time, those were the years when McLuhan found new horizons for his research as testified by a different series of works: *City as Classroom* (McLuhan et al., 1977), an essay about the role of media in the educational processes, *Laws of Media* (McLuhan M. and McLuhan E., 1988), completed and posthumously published by his son Eric, *The Global Village* (McLuhan and Powers, 1989), a collection of writings and notes from the late part of his career, and *Media and Formal Cause* (McLuhan M. and McLuhan E., 2011), recently published by Eric McLuhan as a philosophical commentary with insights on Aristotle and Francis Bacon, Thomas Aquinas, and Gianbattista Vico. These works prioritized aspects of McLuhan's thinking that constituted the background of the research of the Canadian thinker. These works present McLuhan as an original thinker in many ways who was often relegated to a marginal position by specialized literature, despite the fact his work were a result of his attempt to emancipate his research methodologies from the generalist patina of the clichés it was associated with. If we add to these books the works he had previously developed around artistic (McLuhan and Parker, 1968), literary (McLuhan, 1969a), advertising (1951), and philosophical interests (1943), we can observe the truest characteristics of a syncretic thinker, a confident humanist who was interested in the human implications of technology, who promoted a wide-ranging of cultural enterprises, and successfully conveyed a holistic and all-engaging vision. These elements have earned him a place among the most relevant intellectual figures of the twentieth century and rightfully identify him as one of the key authors, if not the main forerunner, of the area of cross-disciplinary studies defined as media ecology.

For an idea of form

The extensive biographical studies of McLuhan grant an impression of an encyclopedic thinker who resists classification and whose insights escape a rigid disciplinary specialism. It was precisely this flexible frame of mind that led him to conceive his studies as based on a systemic approach to knowledge. In contrast to conventional areas of inquiry, he often began his investigations with one of his 'probes' or provocative statements: «Objects are unobservable, only relationships among objects are observable» (Stearn, 1967, p. 260). This is a characteristic element of McLuhan's organic, systemic, and ecological approach.

Although it was only from the late 1960s that he started using the expression media ecology (Gencarelli, 2000, p. 91), many of his previous works already convey an environmental approach to media. In a note in the introduction of *The Gutenberg Galaxy*, he wrote: «There might have been some advantage in substituting for the word "galaxy" the word "environment". Any technology tends to create a new human environment. [...] Technological environments are not merely passive containers but are active processes that reshape people and other technologies alike» (McLuhan, 1962, p. 20). A few years after that, in relation to the celebrated aphorism "the medium is the message", he would again articulate this new stance: «Environments are not just containers, but are processes that change the content totally. New media are the new environments. This is why the media are the message» (1967a, p. 165). This almost sounds as an invitation to acknowledge media as more than empty or neutral vessels that merely channel a content, as they interact and interfere with said content. In *The Medium is the Massage* he also wrote: «It is impossible to understand social and cultural changes without a knowledge of the workings of media» (McLuhan and Fiore, 1967, p. 26). In other words, the reference to the concept of environment in its metaphorical value seems to be a constant concern for McLuhan. Such a concern leads him to unmask once more the fallacy of the idea of the media's neutrality. Medium and message are inseparable precisely because the medium is an active container, a formative process. In other words, for McLuhan the medium is an open, dynamic, active, and pervasive environment.

The systemic and procedural logic inherent in the environmental metaphor used by McLuhan is also reflected in another conceptual combination, the idea of "mosaic", that is ultimately part of his method and specific writing style (Lamberti, 2012). There is, however, an element that has not been adequately explored by scholars of McLuhan, one that is closely related to the environmental view of media presented both in his works and in the intellectual tradition of media ecology. This is the idea of *form*, a key concept that transversally runs through McLuhan's entire written ouevre and that once more reveals the literary sensitivity that specifically distinguished him as a scholar. Given its semantic richness, the idea of form also provides insight to the core of McLuhan's encyclopedism as well as to his ecological approach. All in all, the word environment may be considered precisely as a synonym of form, or an active container that can trigger processes of perception and change. It should also be said that, in the peculiar terminology McLuhan uses to describe media— scale, pace, rhythm, archetype, relationships, proportions, patterns, models—there is an echo of the same meaning that is basically at the heart of the idea of form defined by the aesthetical and philosophical tradition (Tatarkiewicz, 1975, p. 225). In addition, there is a further term, *aesthetics*, that underlies the idea of form for McLuhan and is a fundamental tenet in humanistic and philosophical thought.

If one rereads McLuhan's works in the light of this meditation, or of the attempt to survey the relationships between media and senses—the peculiar field of aesthetics—he certainly emerges as the very first academic to propose this connection. For this reason, we should now add one more label to the many, rightly or wrongly, already attached to him—and that is the label of *aesthetologist*. Once McLuhan's aesthetics is rightfully defined as an aesthetics of form, this unconventional professor of English literature who was particularly interested in mass culture must be necessarily induced in the history of aesthetics and be credited for having achieved an extraordinary turning point within which the problems of aesthetic form are reconsidered in relation with the various forms of different media.

In order to survey the relationship between media and the senses, McLuhan starts from the belief that «the insistent operation of media-forms on human sensibility and awareness is an observable and intelligible situation» (McLuhan, 1959a, p. 346). The probe he devised to observe this situation is obviously provocatory and cheeky, and takes the form of a paradox: "the medium is the message" (1964a, p. 29). By using this probe, McLuhan *applies* aesthetics and in doing so plays the role of an aesthetic operator rather than a critic who wants to understand the media forms starting from their effects on perception. As he would write at a later stage: «I am not a "culture critic" because I am not in any way interested in classifying cultural forms. I am a metaphysician, interested in the life of the forms and their surprising modalities» (McLuhan et al., 1987, p. 413). In other words, his approach is pragmatic rather than theoretical. For this reason, McLuhan's approach to form may be defined as an applied aesthetics and thus an aesthetics that is seen through a possibility of dialogical, and never dialectical, mediation; an approach aimed at solving the seeming conflict between senses and intellect, intuition and reason, subject and object, within the same critical horizon, in order to understand the mutual connections between sensory and cognitive spheres. McLuhan plays with words in describing this interplay: «This image of a unified *ratio* among the senses was long held to be a mark of our *ratio*nality» (McLuhan, 1964a, p. 74).

This tangle of perceptions and conceptions can only be unraveled by considering another mainstay of McLuhan's thought, the notion of experience, and more precisely, the particular perceptive condition defined by the aesthetic experience, or the intensification and full display of the entire sensory apparatus: «Rationality or consciousness is itself a *ratio* or proportion among the sensuous components of experience, and is not something "added" to such sense experience» (p. 114). Therefore, there is a specific element in the way human beings behave and interact within our environment that is inherent in the aesthetic experience, or trying to apprehend the world's material reality and changing it by acting and relying on practical (*prassein* means acting) or ethical (*ethos*: habit, behaviour, etc.) nature. It is a condition of complete involvement with the world, and its material, implemental and symbolic dimension. As such, it defines a pragmatic horizon made of choices, and reliance on instruments having a precise degree of validity and functionality. Therefore, the ethical and behavioural dimension also appears to be connected to the forms of aesthetic experience more than it is perhaps to the cognitive sphere. As McLuhan argues: «Everybody experiences far more than he understands. Yet, it is experience, rather than understanding, that influences behaviour, especially in collective matters of media and technology, where the individual is almost inevitably unaware of their effect upon him» (p. 285). Ultimately, McLuhan's aesthetic approach highlights the media's peculiar function in shaping experience.

The medium's shaping function

One of the first specific features of McLuhan's aesthetics may be defined by the following statement: media as the experience of forms. McLuhan makes his purpose clear in the following declaration of intent: «The *Gutenberg Galaxy* is intended to trace the ways in which the *forms* of experience and of mental outlook and expression have been modified, first by the phonetic alphabet and then by printing» (1962, p. 1). About the issue of technological revolution, when McLuhan wonders, via Peter Drucker, «What happened to bring about the basic change in attitudes, beliefs, and values which released it?" (p. 3), the answer he finds is explicitly stated to be the media of our communication—the function of a process of reframing the human experience. The media of our communication shapes human experience. This is what McLuhan defines as an actual "revolution of forms" (p. 2), an insight he reaches by following the research about orality and literacy developed by Milmann Parry, Eric Havelock, and, later on, further expanded by Jack Goody (§ 5.3) and Walter Ong (§ 3.3), among others. But McLuhan is not satisfied with merely understanding the genesis of such forms. He goes well beyond that by relying on another of his intellectual references, Harold Innis (§ 3.1). McLuhan extends the principle of the revolution of forms by investing all media with no exception, each in its own way, with a power that effectively shapes individual experience and at the same time transforms culture in general terms: «Just as a metaphor transforms and transmits experience so do the media» (McLuhan, 1964a, p. 59). In this sense, he particularly acknowledges Harold Innis who «was the first person to hit upon the *process* of change as implicit in the *forms* of media technology» (1962, p. 51).

His argument developed about the forms of human experience sheds further light on McLuhan's definition of medium. This is explored in one of his last works that would later form the core of *Laws of Media* (McLuhan M. and McLuhan E., 1988), almost closing the circle of a career that perhaps ended too soon. A few years earlier, he had explained: «I am talking about media as a larger entity of information and perception which forms our thoughts, structures our experience, and determines our views of the world about us» (McLuhan, 1975, p. 75). Anything may act as a medium as long as it performs a *shaping* function—or, exhibits a form that *shapes*. In other words, in the relationship humans have with the world, or in the relationship between subject and environment that was so important from pragmatist perspectives, the medium should not be viewed as a thing, an object, an instrument, an artifact, but rather as a function, or a functional process that shapes human experience, a function of the interaction and mediation between humans and their environment. In order to understand this, one should simply read again some of McLuhan's most quoted words by replacing the word message with the word function. The result is «the "message"—the function—of any medium or technology is the change of scale or pace or pattern that it introduces into human affairs» (McLuhan, 1964a, p. 8). But recognizing that the medium is a function that can shape experience is not enough. McLuhan's method of inquiry aimed to understanding *how* this happens. His skills as a man of letters and his inherent passion for art lead him to highlight the relations and connections between daily experience and the different forms of expression in order to understand their complex relationship.

By relying on an example borrowed from the world of art, McLuhan explains that the medium penetrates human experience—or how it is formed—through the sphere of the senses. In this regard, in a little- known passage, he writes: «The meaning of a work of art, as the artists of past centuries can tell us, has nothing to do with what you think about it. It has to do with its action upon you. It is a form: it acts upon you. It invades your senses. It re-structures your outlook. It completely changes your attitudes, your wavelengths. So our attitudes, our sensibilities are completely altered by new forms, regardless of what we think about them» (McLuhan, 1959b, p. 38). Therefore, for McLuhan, the medium shapes human experience to the extent that it pierces through the boundaries of our senses, and in so doing generates a fully aesthetic experience, as it is generally the case in the world of art, although it also occurs in other cases. McLuhan's goal was to expand the ground of aesthetics to include the media within his area of concern.

Forming the five sense sensorium

The notion of aesthetic experience acquires an additional meaning also in the light of the relationship between media forms and what McLuhan defines as *sensorium* (McLuhan, 1961), a term he borrows from Scholasticism. Understanding media, first of all, means understanding their sensory modes, how they act on the human sensorium, or on our constructs of perception and awareness. Ultimately, the well-known distinction between *hot* and *cool* media (1964a, p. 42) is most simply explained as a distinction between different sensory modes: one is linear, homogeneous, visual, the other is circular, immersive, tactile. McLuhan chooses to follow the insight of applying the theories of the forms of visual representation to the forms of media. As a result, even the two "galaxies"—Gutenberg and Marconi—or his notions of *visual space* and *acoustic space* (McLuhan, Carpenter, 1960; McLuhan, 1969b, 1969c), emerge as two possible forms of sensory configuration. The same may be said about the conceptual couples cliché/archetype (McLuhan, Watson, 1970) and figure/ground (McLuhan M. and McLuhan E., 1988).

McLuhan believes that media reshape the form of the five senses: «Any new medium alters the existing sense-ratios and proportions» (McLuhan, 1961, p. 47). The words "ratio" and "proportion" not coincidentally used by McLuhan evoke the meaning of form in the Greek sense of *schêma*, or *habitus* in Latin. In other words, McLuhan argues that media are «forms that shape and reshape our perceptions. That is what I have meant all along by saying "the medium is the message"» (McLuhan, 1967b, p. 160). To reach these conclusions, he once more relies on his artistic sensitivity and an unparalleled intellectual voraciousness that led him to find a truly brilliant array of insights in the so-called Viennese School: the fathers of the aesthetics of form, Wölfflin, Hildebrand, Panofsky, and their heirs Giedion, Kepes, and Gombrich (McLuhan, Parker, 1968). Furthermore, as McLuhan argues, the forms of the sensorium concern more than human individuals, as they are historically and culturally determined. The shaping action of media upon the human sensorium results in a collective, historical, and social change; an anthropological transformation of the sensorial and cultural lives as interwoven entities. This is what he tries to define by using the meaningful expression of cultural ecology that, as he argues, «has a reasonably stable base in the human sensorium, and that any extension of the sensorium by technological dilation has a quite appreciable effect in setting up new ratios or proportions among all the senses» (McLuhan, 1962, p. 64). At this point, it becomes clear how the idea of cultural ecology in connection with the senses would be developed within the field of cross-disciplinary studies of media ecology (Morrison, 2000).

By reasoning in terms of cultural ecology—in a way that is not so different from how the concept was developed in the anthropological field, in particular by Julian Steward (§ 4.3)—McLuhan establishes the foundation of an environmental type of logic that could be applied to the study of media. The shaping function of media are indeed rooted in a sort of sensory and cognitive background, a perceptual environment that shapes and determines an array of formative processes that are as hidden as powerful, deep, influential, an actual ecology of forms, fundamentally described in the note to the *Gutenberg Galaxy*: «Any technology tends to create a new human environment» (McLuhan, 1962, p. 20).

One last consideration that places McLuhan's thought at the root of media ecology's intellectual tradition affects instead the systemic nature of human expressive forms, or these forms viewed in their entirety. These forms act and mutually interact according to a logic of coexistence. No form is isolated from the others. No medium acts independently. The eco-systemic nature of form follows a logic of interdependence. As a result, the various forms of media create one complex and multifaceted environment, an expressive network, a constantly changing dynamic background.

This series of meditations about form viewed as a transformative, relational, invisible, and systemic process, or as a media aesthetics based on an ecological system, reveal the world of media forms as a world of always complex forms, as McLuhan observed early on (McLuhan, 1959b, p. 38). Such complexity results from the plural nature of media forms, from their layering, hybridization, and transformation that, while occurring under our eyes, remains in many ways invisible, hidden, or otherwise covert (as our aquatic friends discovered at the outset of this book). And it is precisely this environmental nature, inherent in the forms of media, that makes them somehow invisible. Ultimately, based on the approach of media ecology, the ecosystem of media should be viewed precisely from that revolution of the forms presciently argued by McLuhan, a revolution that has constantly and silently been occurring in human culture. Exploring media as environments means capturing the very essence of the shaping action that any cultural, social, human environment performs: media ecology therefore offers a comprehensive perspective to understanding something more about the contemporary human condition, shaped and fashioned by the ever new forms of media and the systemic interplay of their form.

Marshall McLuhan's main works
The Classical Trivium (1943)
The Mechanical Bride (1951)
The Gutenberg Galaxy (1962)
Understanding Media (1964)
The Medium is the Massage (1967)
Through the Vanishing Point (1968), with Harley Parker
The Interior Landscape (1969)
Counterblast (1969), with Harley Parker
Culture is our Business (1970)
From Cliché to Archetype (1970), with W. Watson
Take Today, (1972), with Barrington Nevitt
City as Classroom (1977), with Eric McLuhan and Kathryn Hutchon
Laws of Media (1988) posthumous, with Eric McLuhan
The Global Village (1989) posthumous, with Bruce R. Powers
Media and Formal Cause (2011) posthumous, with Eric McLuhan
The Future of the Library (2015) posthumous, with Robert K. Logan

Further readings
Carey J.W. (1967), "Harold Innis and Marshall McLuhan", *Antioch Review*, 27, 1, pp. 5-39.
Carey J.W. (1998), "Marshall McLuhan. Genealogy and Legacy", *Canadian Journal of Communication*, 23, 3, pp. 293-306.
Cavell R. (2002), *McLuhan in Space. A Cultural Geography*, Univ. of Toronto Press, Toronto.
Fitzgerald J. (2001), *Marshall McLuhan. Wise Guy*, XYZ Pub, Montreal.
Gordon W.T. (1997), *Marshall McLuhan. Escape into Understanding*, BasicBooks, New York.
Gordon W.T. (2010), *McLuhan. A guide for the perplexed*, Continuum, New York.
Grosswiler P. (1998), *The Method is the Message. Rethinking McLuhan Through Critical Theory*, Black Rose Books, Montreal.
Lamberti E. (2012), *Marshall McLuhan's Mosaic: Probing the Literary Origins of Media Studies*, University of Toronto Press, Toronto.
Levinson P. (1999), *Digital McLuhan. A Guide to the Information Millennium*, Routledge, New York.

Logan R.K. (2013), *McLuhan Misunderstood*, Key Publishing House, Toronto.
Marchand P. (1989), *Marshall McLuhan. The Medium and the Messenger*, Random House, Toronto.
Marchessault J. (2005), *Marshall McLuhan. Cosmic media*, Sage, London.
McLeod Rogers, J., Taylor, C.G., Whalen, T., eds. (2015), *Finding McLuhan. The mind, the man, the message*, University of Regina Press, Regina, Saskatchewan.
McLuhan E., Szklarek J., eds. (1999), *The Medium and the Light: Reflections on Religion*, Stoddart, Toronto.
McLuhan E., Zingrone Z., eds. (1995), *Essential McLuhan*, BasicBooks, New York.
Molinaro M., McLuhan C. e Toye W., eds. (1987), *Letters of Marshall McLuhan*, Oxford University Press, Toronto-New York.
Morra L.M., Moss J.G., eds. (2004), *At the speed of light there is only illumination. A reappraisal of Marshall McLuhan*, Univ. of Ottawa Press, Ottawa.
Morrison J.C. (2006), "Marshall McLuhan. The Modern Janus", in Lum C.M.K., ed, *Perspectives on Culture, Technology and Communication*, Hampton Press, Cresskill, NJ, pp. 163-200.
Powe B.W. (2014), *Marshall McLuhan and Northrop Frye. Apocalypse and Alchemy*, University of Toronto Press, Toronto.
Rosenthal R., ed. (1968), *McLuhan Pro & Con*, Funk & Wagnalls, New York.
Sanderson G., McDonald F., eds. (1988), *Marshall McLuhan: The Man and His Message*, Fulcrum Publishing, Golden CO.
Stearn G.E. (1967), *McLuhan. Hot & Cool*, Signet Books, New York.
Strate S. (2008), "Studying Media as Media. Marshall McLuhan and the Media Ecology Approach", *MediaTropes*, 1, pp. 127-142.
Strate L. e Wachtel E., eds. (2005), *The Legacy of McLuhan*, Hampton, Cresskill, NJ.
Theall D.F. (2001), *The virtual Marshall McLuhan*, McGill-Queen's University Press, Montreal.
Willmott G. (1996), *McLuhan, or Modernism in Reverse*, University of Toronto Press, Toronto.

Documentary films
McLuhan's Wake (2002), Kevin McMahon, David Sobelman.
Extraordinary Canadians: Marshall McLuhan (2017), CBC.

3.3 Walter Ong and the ecology of the word

The American Jesuit Walter J. Ong (1912-2003) is the academic who should be credited for systematizing the particular section of media ecology aimed at understanding the development of human culture starting from the communication dimension by particularly addressing the relations between forms of verbal language and writing processes. A historian of culture and religions, an expert of rhetoric and Romance philology, and a brilliant interpreter of human history, Walter Ong embodies the image of the syncretic scholar who effortlessly moved in the wide realm of the humanities. His works address a variety of fields including literature, linguistics, psychology, and anthropology among others. Due to his flexibility and argumentative clarity, his approach represents a fundamental reference in the wide realm of North American media and communication studies.

Ong was born in Kansas City, Missouri, where he entered the Society of Jesuits very young and was ordained a priest in 1946. Between 1938 and 1941 he studied at Saint Louis University where he graduated in philosophy and theology, and met Marshall McLuhan (§ 2.2), then a young English literature professor. This encounter would be a fundamental event for both, who were more or less of the same age and established a connection of deep intellectual understanding and mutual respect (Ong, 1989; Farrel, 2000). After Ong graduated with a dissertation about the British modernist poet and Jesuit Gerard Hopkins, McLuhan himself encouraged his promising student to continue his academic training at Harvard. In that prestigious university, under the guidance of the American historian Perry Miller, Ong produced an in-depth study of the birth of modern logic and on Renaissance rationalism by studying the 16th century French theologian Peter Ramus, following a hint McLuhan had given him years before. The research became his very first work, *Ramus. Method, and the Decay of Dialogue* (Ong, 1958). Since his move to Harvard, Ong's intellectual activity continued ceaselessly. In 1954, he was appointed professor of English literature at Saint Louis University. Besides teaching and attending to his daily religious functions, he would play an active role within several cultural and literary institutions. In 1966-1967 he served on the White House Task Force on Education that reported to President Lyndon Johnson. He later received several prestigious national and international awards and acknowledgements including his election as a Fellow of the American Academy of Arts and Sciences and his appointment as Chevalier dans l'Ordre des Palmes Académiques by the French Government. The number of collections of writings devoted to his work (Gronbeck et al., 1991; Weeks and Hoogestraat, 1998; Farrel and Soukup, 2012) testify to the relevance of Walter Ong's intellectual heritage not just within the intellectual tradition of media ecology but also in the wider realm of philosophical studies.

Ong developed his activity as an essayist over about forty years with over 450 items including books and essays, now collected in a substantial archive at Saint Louis University, where many manuscripts have been made available online. However, the main core of his work is constituted of three main books: *The Presence of the Word* (1967), *Interfaces of the Word* (1977) and *Orality and Literacy* (1982), published between the late 1960s and the early 1980s.

In the beginning was the word

The fundamental assumption underlying Ong's research is the power of communication media to shape human thought in any historical age; in other words, to contribute to the long-term transformation of humanity's mental and cognitive structures—defined by Ong as "human psychodynamics" (Ong, 1982, p. 59)—and in turn to trigger a sweeping change in social and cultural processes. In Ong's vision, the history of human culture is closely related to the history of communication forms and, in particular, to the changes in verbal expression and language, or what he defines as «the transformations of the word» (Ong, 1967). In *Interfaces of the Word* he writes: «Major developments, and very likely all major developments, in culture and consciousness, are related, often in unexpected intimacy, to the evolution of the word from primary orality to its present state» (Ong, 1977, p. 21). Ong introduces an original periodization of the different phases of human culture, articulated across about six millennia of history and divided into three precises phases of verbalization, three major anthropological cycles of communication forms.

The first phase—more or less coinciding with the archaic ages, from the appearance of language onwards—is defined as *primary orality*, or pre-literacy phase, the long preparation that led to the invention of writing. This is followed by the phase of *literacy* starting with the so-called chirographic revolution, or the appearance of writing. Its apex would coincide with the introduction of movable type print during the Renaissance and its later developments in the modern age. The third phase, defined as *secondary orality*, post-literacy, or post-literary phase, begins with the so-called electronic age inaugurated by the developments of electrophysics in the late 19th century. Consolidated by the invention of the wireless telegraph in the early 20th century, this phase continued for the entire century with the propagation of the mass media and information technology.

Across these three phases, the expression forms of the word change but are never mutually exclusive; they cross-breed, or add to and complete each other. However, the particular transformation in the structures of the human sensory system occurring in each of these phases invariably highlights one or more perceptive factors closely connected to the prevailing communication forms. Therefore, every anthropological cycle corresponds to a different configuration of the human sensory sphere, following a principle of «historicization of the sensorium» (Barilli, 1970). This has indeed a deep impact on human psychodynamics, or on the cognitive components and thought and knowledge structures. Therefore, any new psycho-perceptive configuration, any revolution of the senses, has the power to directly impact on the characters of knowledge that are transmitted.

Ong's insights on the phase of primary orality are deeply rooted in the area of studies developed around the so-called Homeric question introduced by **Milman Parry** (1902-1935), a North American Hellenist scholar, through a series of works published between 1928 and 1935 (Parry, 1971) and later collected by his son Adam after Parry's premature death. Ong thought that Parry had effectively used the methods of ethnology and linguistics to find a direct connection between the expressive forms of Homeric poetry and the main features of oral culture. The use of standardized formulas and recurrent thematic repertoires at Homer's time—a sort of narrative encyclopedia of collective behaviours—was directly connected to the need to stabilize the organization models of the poetic process. Parry shed a light on the Homeric poems' oral nature and showed how the formal structures of Greek epic somehow resulted from the inherent and peculiar features of oral culture and thinking. Rather than works of writing they were works of memory that insisted on the aural rather than visual dimension. All of these arguments were Ong's starting point in providing a convincing description of the typical features of oral cultures.

In the phase that he defined as primary orality, the sensory component of hearing plays a major role and therefore influences the cognitive processes of the archaic, tribal, or non-alphabetized human subject. Ong also defines this phase as aural culture to highlight listening rather than verbalizing processes. Therefore, in archaic, tribal, or illiterate cultures, the spoken word, as an oral-aural expressive form, occurs in its original and natural habitat—the world of sound generated by human phonation—and reveals itself as an event that is closely inherent to the world and the time of the present. On the other hand, in its being ephemeral, instantaneous, and transient, the spoken word acquires the features of a magical ritual, a mysterious spell that impacts on the forms of human experience. It is the magic of the world that becomes gesture, action, invocation and as such as elusive, mysterious, secret, and sometimes irrational. Therefore, in oral culture, human beings —the knowing subject—and what surrounds them (the object of perception) are closely connected by their concurrent belonging to the world. Similarly, knowledge lives in the present time, in simultaneity and instantaneity, and similar to the Homeric era only memory has the power to preserve or transmit part of it through the reliance on structured formulas or mnemonic devices: «you know what you can recall» (Ong, 1982, p. 61). During the phase of primary orality, memory is therefore conceived as something that is inherent to human conscience, and liable to the wear of time—*verba volant*, as Latin speakers used to say—and for this reason it should be preserved by using formulaic and rhythmic structures that facilitate the development of the narrative process

(Biason, 2006). Oral culture, moreover, promotes the sharing of stories and other narrative communication. A social and, more specifically, collective connection is therefore facilitated because, due to the absence of writing, knowledge can only reveal itself and settle through aural, tactile and bodily interaction; a empathic and relational exchange.

A new life for the word

Ong's description of the peculiar features of the second phase, the phase of literacy, is in many ways entwined with the concurrent studies of **Eric Havelock** (1903-1988). A British philologist and classicist who later moved to Northern America, Havelock had studied the deep changes that accompanied the passage from oral to literate culture in Greece, and demonstrated how the process of development of rational thinking and the logical-sequential model that led to the birth of Greek philosophy and the supremacy of its civilization was closely connected to the internalization of emergent writing practices. In other words, writing facilitated the release of the human mind's cognitive structures from the reliance on the collective encyclopedia of gestures that underlies oral culture. Therefore, literacy had promoted the development of a new type of thinking that could be defined as alphabetical, literate, or more generally visual. In brief, for Havelock (1963) the revolution triggered by writing in ancient Greece led to the birth of the so-called alphabetic mind—«a gift of Hellenistic tradition to the modern world» (1986b)—or a new thinking subject who broke free from the previous models of oral culture by acquiring a new approach to the visualization of knowledge provided by writing. Writing implies radically different forms of thought. In fact, analytical thought cannot even be communicated, or even thought, in a culture that is not aware of alphabetic writing. The transition from the phase of orality to that of literacy in Western human history, just like the difference between the sensory and cognitive components of the two cultures, would be the object of sweeping research projects developed during the same years in an anthropological vein by the British academic Jack Goody (1977; 1987; § 5.3). Therefore, the hypotheses proposed by Havelock starting from an historical-literary point of view were further confirmed by Goody's research on then-modern illiterate cultures of the African continent (Goody and Watt, 1963). Ong was inspired by Havelock's research, confirmed by Goody, to define the distinctive features of the second phase of human culture based on the practice of writing.

In the phase of literacy, it is the sense of sight that prevails. The written word, as a visual expression form, in a certain sense changes nature. When it becomes a sign, it acquires a spatial dimension and with it the features of a technology, in a process defined by Ong as «the technologizing of the word» in *Orality and Literacy* (Ong, 1982, p. 123). Otherwise said, writing reifies the spoken word and transforms it into something that is solid, visible, and material, and puts the literate in a condition of non-return: it is impossible to observe a word without thinking about its meaning. Ong explains that «writing restructures consciousness» (p. 119). This deep transformation of human cognitive condition implies an artifactual, man-made, technological component: «All major advances in consciousness depend on technological transformations and implementations of the word» (Ong, 1977, p. 49).

Ong argues that technologies «are not mere exterior aids but also interior transformations of consciousness, and never more than when they affect the word» (Ong, 1982, p. 124). Therefore, writing becomes a technology of the word as it transforms sound into space, it transforms the *now* and *here* into *always* and *anywhere* that separates and removes the thinker/speaker from the thought/expressed and from the listener. As a consequence, knowledge does not live exclusively in the social and cultural memory carried by the individual and collective memory that is typical of orality. Written documents have the power to preserve or transmit such memory that, being now an exterior fact, is saved from the wear of time and therefore acquires a historical dimension. As an extension of collective memory, writing therefore creates the very idea of history. Through the written word, the communication event is not merely something that occurs in the uniqueness of the present moment but becomes a fact that lives on in time according to a linear model that settles in the past and can constantly be evoked from the past. Similarly, the distance between subject and object of perception increases in space and time. However, in a first stage of literacy—more or less the centuries between the Classical antiquity and the Middle Age—the written word was still experienced in its oral dimension. Manuscripts are hardly accessible and only used by a restricted circle of academics and men of letters, and texts are read out loud or acquired by lip-reading in a limited few centres of production and propagation of knowledge such as the convents and early universities. The zenith of the process of visualization of the word in space would indeed be reached only with the propagation of printing during the Renaissance, and subsequently through the large-scale production of books that, unlike manuscripts, established once and for all styles, formats, and conventions of writing, and actually expanded the possibilities of access to and propagation of knowledge.

Ong's arguments about the typographic phase of literacy was quickly embraced and developed by Elizabeth Eisenstein in a brilliant essay entitled *The Printing Press as an Agent of Change* (Eisenstein, 1979). Following on the footsteps of Ong, Havelock, and McLuhan, Eisenstein demonstrates how major religious, political, and economic changes of the modern age actually occur on the backdrop of an even wider, but in many ways hidden, invisible, sudden revolution—an "unacknowledged revolution" (p. 66)—that can be connected to the invention and propagation of printing. The development of modernity is related to the birth of the modern book thanks to which the process of knowledge becomes an eminently individual, internalized, and private matter, the reflection of a mental attitude that promotes interior perception, critical elaboration, introspection, and analytical thinking, therefore intensifying individualism, the Cartesian *cogito* and the development of the self (Flichy, 1995, p. 58). All this does not imply a receding social and community dimension, and not even an increasing distance between the individual and their relational context. It rather means, as Ong argues, that, by promoting the development of interior consciousness and the sense of the self, writing actually «fosters a more conscious interaction between persons» (Ong, 1982, p. 245).

Return to orality

The third phase, the phase of secondary or post-typographic orality, marks a further reconfiguration of the human sensory and cognitive sphere. In advancing these arguments, Ong's theses intersect those of McLuhan (§ 3.2), all the while preserving their independence and inherent coherence due to an approach that is altogether more cautious and refined than that of the Canadian media guru (Havelock, 1986a, p. 43). Anyway, due to the better reception it elicited from historians and other scholars, both in North America and in Europe, Ong's work helped strengthen and propagate the brilliant insights proposed by McLuhan, particularly during the 1970s and 1980s: indeed, if the phrase «Gutenberg Galaxy» (McLuhan, 1962) became common among experts in the field it was probably due to the Jesuit academic's efforts.

During the phase of secondary, post-literate, or post-typographic orality that corresponds to the so-called electronic age, there is a return to verbal expression forms, or a revival of the word's sound dimension. Indeed, Ong defines this stage as a «return to orality» (Ong, 1982, p. 21) that, through the telegraph, the cinema, and above all radio and television, is again based on aural experience and its related cognitive aspects. In the electronic age, the word comes back as sound, or a sound action. For this reason, it promotes a newly found enveloping, embracing, and immersive sense of presence and involvement in a way that is not so different from what happened during the ancient tribal age. Indeed, the verbalization of sound in the electronic media environment reinstates an even more powerful version of the oral-aural condition based on the communication event, the word-event. The acoustic component, the new orality of the electronic media and their reliance on the aural sphere revive the ritual dimension of communication, that which is experienced collectively through interaction, sharing and exchange.

Viewing communication forms in their ritual dimension also means overcoming an idea of communication that is basically transmission of content. The sound component of verbal expression implies a communication model of a relational type. It is in relation that communication occurs. It is the ability to create or simulate a relational environment of inherence, contact, and proximity that leads the oral communication forms to promote new thought models. Ong writes: «Each of the so-called "media" [...] makes possible thought processes inconceivable before. The "media" are more significantly within the mind than outside it» (Ong, 1977, p. 52).

However, during the electronic age, the word only reconquers part of the original and archaic habitat that surrounded the tribal, or illiterate, humans as it coexists with the visual dimension of space that accompanies writing and print—two forms particularly rooted in current cultural and social processes—and confronts the potential of sound and visual recording technologies (starting with the invention of the phonograph, *verba* actually *manent*) and of data storage, that obviously transforms words in retrievable and transmissible documents, similar to the forms of documentality typical of the literacy phase. Basically, the return to orality in the contemporary age is complicated by the simultaneous presence of the forms of writing and print developed in the modern age. Similarly, there is a simultaneous complication in the process of configuration of the sensory and the human cognitive sphere that therefore require a new approach in order to fully recognize both the formative action performed by writing and print on the current forms of thought, and the tension between orality and writing in the contemporary world. The simultaneous presence of both components in the third phase described by Ong may therefore be understood starting from this awareness, thus from the recognition of the complex balance between the different expression forms of communication, first of all, by accepting that there is no antagonism between them. The author indeed points out that: «the media in their succession do not cancel out one another but build on one another. When man began to write, he did not cease talking. [...]. When print was developed, man did not stop writing [...]. Technological society in the electronic age cannot exist without vast quantities of writing and print» (Ong, 1967, p. 103). Ong's undisputedly relevant role within the intellectual tradition of media ecology is mainly due to his ability to recognize this particular relationship of reciprocity between orality and writing in the electronic age without any subordination of one to the other and, as well, his attempt to recognize the complexity of the dynamics between the two within an overall understanding of human history.

The interaction between the two communication forms of orality and writing in the electronic age frames the development of the three ages of the word described by Ong within an organic process of understanding of human development. He writes: «Orality-literacy dynamics enter integrally into the modern evolution of consciousness toward both greater interiorization and greater openness» (Ong, 1982, p. 246). In this process, each communication form performs a particular role in adjusting and balancing the human sensory components according to a verb-acoustic-visual model (Gronbeck, 2006, p. 348), determined every time by multiple interactions between communication and thought forms, that could be defined as an actual ecological model. The history of communication, in the periodization defined by Ong, is therefore the history of the constant adaptation of human thought to a constant, environmental formative process that, while tending to a balance, is constantly changing. The spiritual meaning that Ong attributes to the return to the word lies in the redefinition of the features of the social and cultural environment starting with the articulation of a new concept of individual. In this aspect lies the ecological and humanistic approach that Ong's work helped systematize. Every time the media environment changes, human beings are forced to perceptively adapt to it by reorienting our own sensory apparatus. This effort deeply impacts on the structures of human thought that in turn determine new cultural orientations in the existing communication forms. Indeed, even cultures «vary greatly in their exploitation of the various senses and in the way in which they relate their conceptual apparatus to the various senses» (Ong, 1967, p. 9).

In Ong's work, the endeavours of the word, narrated in order to describe the processes of adaptation and reorientation of humanity, become even more intense in the contemporary media environment. In one of his last contributions, he wrote: «The age in which human life and technology so massively and intimately interact, can well be styled not only in the information age and the age of interpretation, but, perhaps, even more inclusively, in principle an age of total interconnectedness» (Ong, 2002, p. 5). In this passage we implicitly find a far from marginal component of Ong's thought, a holism of religious inflection reflected in his belonging to the Jesuit order that draws his focus to the concept of the word—the verb in Koine Greek Christian tradition *logos*—that transcends human life itself. *The Presence of the Word* ended with these words: «The mystery of sound is [...] the most productive of understanding and unity, the most personally human, and in this sense closest to the divine» (Ong, 1967, p. 364). Media ecology follows this line of reasoning: imagining a fundamental coherence, a consistent and dynamic balance based on which everything is interconnected, and discovering, in a certainly more secular perspective, the magical and secret role of the word in the processes of internalization and openness of human consciousness.

Walter Ong's main works
Ramus. Method, and the Decay of Dialogue (1958)
The presence of the word (1967)
Rhetoric, romance, and technology (1971)
Why talk? (1973)
Interfaces of the word (1977)
Fighting for life (1981)
Orality and literacy (1982)

Further readings
Farrel T.J. (2000), *Walter Ong's Contributions to Cultural Studies. The Phenomenology of the Word and I-thou Communication*, Hampton Press, Cresskill, NJ.
Farrel T.J., Soukup P.A., eds. (2012), *Of Ong and Media Ecology. Essays in Communication, Composition, and Literary Studies*, Hampton Press, New York.
Farrel T.J., Soukup P.A., eds. (2002), *An Ong reader. Challenges for further inquiry*, Hampton Press, Cresskill, NJ.
Gronbeck B.E., Farrel T.J., Soukup P.A., eds. (1991), *Media, Consciousness and Culture. Explorations of Walter Ong's Thought*, Sage, Thousand Oaks, CA.
Gronbeck B.E. (2006), "The Orality-Literacy Theorems and Media Ecology", in Lum C.M.K., ed., *Perspectives on Culture, Technology and Communication: The Media Ecology Tradition*, Hampton Press, Cresskill, NJ, pp. 335-265.
Van den Berg S., Walsh, T.M., eds. (2011), *Language, culture, and identity. The legacy of Walter J. Ong*, S.J, Hampton Press, Cresskill, NJ.
Weeks D.L., Hoogestraat J.A., eds. (1998), *Time, Memory and the Verbal Arts: Essays on the Thought of Walter Ong*, Associated University Presses, Cranbury, NJ.

4. Pioneering schools and thinkers

The intellectual schools based in the cultural environments of New York and Toronto owed their development to the converging paths of a host of prominent academics who perpetually challenged North American frontiers of knowledge. By consolidating the network of relations between disciplines, approaches, and visions then flourishing around the major American universities, these flows of exchange effectively helped define the general theoretical frame of media ecology.

The key points of these borderline flows can be recognized by using once more the concept of "school", although, as mentioned before, it should be used with caution and in a highly informal way. Besides the New York and Toronto schools, the intellectual tradition of North American media ecology embraces at least three other major schools: the School of urban sociology established in Chicago between the nineteenth and twentieth century (§ 4.1), not coincidentally also known as the Ecological School; the Palo Alto School (§ 4.2), established during the 1950s in California around the issues of human communication viewed in a relational perspective; and the so-called Boas school (§ 4.3) that benefitted from the contribution of a group of experts of anthropology and cultural relativism. These three schools are only the articulations of a movement that extends well beyond mere labels and is most dynamically expressed by a host of key representatives. Therefore, media ecology embraces major thinkers who belonged to the philosophical family of North American pragmatism such as Dewey and Cooley (§ 4.1), a unique intellectual giant such as Gregory Bateson (§ 4.2), and a broadminded anthropologists such as Edward Hall (§ 4.3).

In addition, there are many others who played an important role in this process by acting as *trait d'union* between different schools and intellectual environments. One of these, and perhaps the most exemplary in this sense, was Erving Goffman (§ 4.2), who studied first in Toronto with Charles Hart and Ray Birdwhistell, and later in Chicago with the second generation of members of the Chicago School by following the approach of symbolic interactionism. He was also in touch with Bateson in San Francisco, with the exponents of second cybernetics in New York, and with the Mental Research Institute of Palo Alto, California.

Finally, there is **James W. Carey** (1934-2006), a key thinker who should be remembered for clarifying with his stringent and clever interpretive sensibility the intellectual development of North American media and communication studies. He was a prolific author, close to the approach of the Chicago School (Subtil, 2008) who, although gifted with a unique investigative autonomy, successfully combined a wide array of paradigms within a constantly coherent vision that would result in insightful interpretations and innovative proposals. Carey's *Communication as Culture* (1989) is a cornerstone for the understanding of the different interpretive models used to frame communication in the second half of the twentieth century, both by arguing a so-called ritual view of communication closer to the ecological approach and by providing a brilliant interpretation of the pragmatist roots of North American communication studies and the role of media in contemporary society according to a wide range of authors, from Innis to Mumford, from McLuhan to Goffman (Carey, 1967, 1981, 1989, 1998). For this reason, Carey may be considered a major interpreter of the intellectual tradition of media ecology.

4.1 The Chicago School and urban ecology

As the cradle of North American sociology, a crossroads of economical and philosophical knowledge, Chicago is one of the essential milestones in the process that led media ecology to become an independent and, in many ways, original study field (despite being based on well-established intellectual traditions). One of said traditions is commonly known as the Chicago School, and can be considered a primary foundation of media ecology in which focus is directed to the environmental elements that impact on the relational processes of humans and social development. The concept according to which individuals and groups are deeply influenced by their environment which in turn plays a major role in the development of human and social processes is one of the benchmarks of the intellectual tradition that grew in Chicago. Indeed, for this reason, the tradition has become well-known as a school of human and social ecology, or simply as the Ecological School.

Countless essays (Hannerz, 1980; Shils, 1991; Hart, 2010), articles (Harvey, 1986; Becker, 1999), collected writings (Burgess and Bogue, 1964; Short, 1971; Rauty, 1999) and encyclopedia entries (Tucker, 2006; Hutchison, 2010) have delineated the history, themes and intellectual development of the Chicago School and assessed them sometimes in contradictory (Harvey, 1986), or even skeptical ways (Castells, 1974; Dear, 2002). Others (Thomas, 1983; Subtil, 2008) have instead recognized the continuing relevance of this tradition. The portrait that emerges from the sheer size of this historiographic production is particularly rich and varied and reflects an extraordinarily relevant cultural heritage that transversally embraces several fields of knowledge, connects diverse minds and insights towards unique and original solutions, and therefore effectively overcomes the individualistic and fragmented understanding of reality that had been prevalent in social sciences. Besides urban studies and ethnographic research, the Chicago School also explored the complexity of the relations between media and society, culture and communication, and therefore somehow anticipated both the subsequent emergence of British cultural studies and the later development of North American media studies by effectively influencing both areas. It is along this lineage that the convergence and affinity with media ecology becomes clearly recognizable (Lum, 2006, p. 11).

The sociological tradition based in Chicago and the intellectual activity that would give rise to its School started during at the very end of the nineteenth century, at the same time as the local university, established in 1890; and, in particular, of the Department of Sociology and Anthropology, founded two years later. At that time, social research as an academic discipline had just become part of the American university system (Hinkle, 1980; Schubert, 2006). The scientific community of Chicago would soon emerge as the cradle of the rising sociological paradigm, also due to the decisive support of philanthropic institutions and associations that, in funding that kind of urban and territorial scale research, could devote part of their profits to social welfare. The American Journal of Sociology, the very first in this field, was established within the Department in 1895, along with the Sociological Series of the Chicago University Press. This is the academic context that produced some of the most prominent figures of an intellectual tradition that would go on to influence entire generations of scholars.

From pragmatism to interactionism

Within the events that marked the development of sociological research in Chicago in the late nineteenth century, a relevant role was played by the cultural context that effectively supported a cross-disciplinary approach such as the one adopted by the members of the School. At the time, Chicago was not only the outpost of American sociological thought, it was also an important centre for historical-economical studies, as well as one of the most relevant hubs of pragmatism (the then most important philosophical current in Northern America) and of what can be considered as its "applied" variation, social psychology (Dennis, Wartella, 1996; Paglia, 2002).

As regards historical-economic studies, **Thorstein Veblen** (1857-1929) was certainly the most prominent figure in Chicago between 1892 and 1906. In combining economics and human sciences within one vision, Veblen effectively initiated a progressive approach to the study of economic processes that shed new light on the connection between technological, humanistic, and social factors and the mechanisms of distribution of wealth (Veblen, 1899). In the following years, Veblen's innovative and non-conventional ideas had a peculiar impact both on historical-economic research in Chicago (Tilman, 1992; Diggins, 1999) and on thinkers who worked outside that context such as Harold Innis (§ 3.1)—who came to Chicago for a short time to study (Czitrom, 1982, pp. 149-151; Carey, 1989, p. 103; Stamps, 1995, pp. 55-56)—and Lewis Mumford (§ 2.1)—who had known Veblen from New York (Halton, 1995, pp.144-145; Diggins, 1999, p. 91): both connected to the study of media ecology (Strate, 2006; Heyer, 2006).

The influence of the pragmatist tradition on the Chicago School in terms of an original combination of philosophy, sociology, and psychology applied to the understanding of the role of media in social life and of the processes of communication in human interaction can be recognized in at least two major exponents of the school. The first one is **John Dewey** (1859-1952), a well-known interpreter of American pragmatism who worked in Chicago from 1894 when he was appointed head of the Department of Philosophy for about a decade. The years Dewey spent in Chicago were a key period in the pragmatist approach applied to the understanding of social phenomena, both in pedagogical terms—the first Laboratory School was established in Chicago during that period (Harms, DePencier, 1996)—and in terms of communication as a field of study, witnessing the actual gestation of American media studies (Czitrom, 1982, pp. 91; Carey, 1989, p. 13; Hardt, 1992, p. 37; Williams, 2003, p. 32). In such historical contexts, the quick development of modern communication forms—first daily newspapers and later the radio—obviously boosted the reformist impulse that inspired the social research environment.

In line with the stance of William James, another voice of pragmatism, Dewey introduced the notion of experience viewed as an element of continuity between the human mind, our inner world, and our environment in the processes of communication. This is actually a key concept of social psychology, especially as it is interpreted in ecological terms: the individual's mind can only be understood in relation with his environmental context. An excerpt from *Democracy and Education* (Dewey, 1916) summarizes what can be considered an ecological view of communication as the common ground within which social action is shaped. Dewey writes: «Society not only continues to exist *by* transmission, *by* communication, but it may fairly be said to exist *in* transmission, *in* communication. There is more than a verbal tie between the words "common", "community", and "communication". Men live in a community in virtue of the things which they have in common» (Dewey, 1916, p. 1). In other words, in Dewey's view communication processes shape, support, and preserve a certain community or society. Dewey's work helped to introduce in Chicago's intellectual environment a vision that was similar to Spencer's concept of society as an organic entity (Spencer, 1860), although reinterpreted according to a holistic understanding of human thought. According to Dewey, humans and the environment live within one horizon of experience that, through the processes of communication, takes on the ever changing and dynamic forms of action. The latter, indeed «carries with it the sense of the participation and connection with a whole» (Dewey, 1925, p. 143). The bottom line is that Dewey's pragmatism helped researchers in Chicago see the interaction between the individual and their environment, focusing on communication as a key element of social analysis.

Charles H. Cooley (1864-1929) is the second figure who should be credited for providing the philosophical foundation that influenced the intellectual development of the Ecological School. Having studied with John Dewey at the University of Michigan, Cooley developed his own research around the mutual relationship between individuals and society. Only within this delicate process of relations can individual action be fully understood in connection with a comprehensive social framework. The analysis developed by Cooley was indeed based on the key idea of interaction as the central process of social life. Based on this vision, any interaction implies a symbolic exchange and becomes a complex network of culturally channeled conventions. This symbolic network is simply the manifestation of the social environment in relation to which each individual shapes themself. Cooley's ideas resulted in the theoretical orientation later defined as symbolic interactionism (Blumer, 1969; Charon, 1979; Barnes, 2002) that provided Chicago's social research with a fundamental set of conceptual instruments in order to overcome the then-prevailing behaviourist approach. According to symbolic interactionism, individual action is not simply a reaction to external stimuli, as the behaviourist perspective argued. Social action is rather shaped by the creation of shared symbols and meanings to the extent that the respective symbolic environment is effectively the frame within which the human beings activate a range of relational exchange processes. Several members of the Ecological School followed this approach and its influence developed into a perseverant approach that continues to stimulate even recent sociological research (Powell, 2013; Meltzer, Petras, Reynolds, 2014).

Cooley was one of the very first thinkers to apply interactionism to the understanding of communication processes (Jandy, 1942; Cohen, 1982; Czitrom, 1982). In *Human Nature and the Social Order* (Cooley, 1902), he explains the subject's active role in shaping his own environment and defines society as the collective reflection of individual thought. At the same time, the social aspects of communication are recognized for their peculiar function in defining the meaningful changes in human cognitive structure. Along this interpretive line, communication is viewed by Cooley as a relational value that drives both individual and collective action, a sort of natural environment for human thought rather than a mere expressive medium for the circulation of information content. Communication is also viewed as a peculiar development factor of human nature, a mental extension—"the larger mind"—on which society is based, as he argued in *Social Organization* (1909). In Cooley's words, communication is «the mechanism through which human relations exist and develop – all the symbols of the mind, together with the means of conveying them through space and preserving them in time. [...] The more closely we consider this mechanism the more intimate will appear its relation to the inner life of mankind» (p. 69). The multiplicity of communication forms, or media in the dimension of space and time, are also defined as a sort of extension of the human mind, «an organic whole corresponding to the organic whole of human thought; and everything in the way of mental growth has an external existence wherein» (*id.*).

As a demonstration of the interest it raised in the intellectual scene of the time (Hinkle, 1980), the speculative approach inaugurated by Cooley was further developed a few years later, and receive an even warmer reception (Harvey, 1986) by **George H. Mead** (1863-1931), who had also studied with Dewey at the University of Michigan and then moved to Chicago to take up a teaching position.

For these reasons, while indebted with Cooley (Mead, 1930), Mead is considered the primary advocate of symbolic interactionism and social psychology (Flichy, 1996; Barnes, 2002; Schubert, 2006). His most relevant work, *Mind, Self and Society* (Mead, 1934), published after his death, particularly influenced the generation of Chicago researchers that emerged after WWII as well as a host of other thinkers including Clyde Kluckhohn, Edward Hall (§ 4.3), Erving Goffman (§ 4.2), James Carey (1989), variously connected both to the heritage of the Ecological School and to the so-called "invisible circle" (Winkin, 1981) led by Gregory Bateson and to media ecology's intellectual tradition (Flayhan, 2002, p. 6; Barnes, 2002, p. 2; Strate, 2006, p. 59; Lum, 2006, p. 31; Wasser, 2006, p. 255).

The influence of European sociology

Two voices are usually remembered as pioneers of the Chicago School. Both should be credited with introducing currents of German philosophical and sociological research in the lively academic context already animated by the pragmatist approach, therefore bringing together the European and North American traditions that, at the time, were still quite removed from each other. The first one is **Albion W. Small** (1854-1926), founder and director of the Department for over thirty years. After studying in Berlin and Leipzig in close connection with Georg Simmel, he returned to Chicago and established a bridge between the German sociological tradition and the North American scene by translating and publishing several works by Simmel and Weber. Small also founded and was the first chairman of the American Sociological Society and edited the first issues of the Society's official organ, the American Journal of Sociology. His main works, *An Introduction to the Study of Society* (1894), co-authored with George Vincent, and *The Organic Concept of Society* (1895) provided up-and-coming students with a key reference text for understanding and propagating the then emerging systemic approach.

The second pioneer of the School's early years was **William I. Thomas** (1863-1947), one of the first students to emerge from the Department itself. After studying in Berlin and Gottingen,

Small invited Thomas to teach in Chicago where he immediately emerged as a brilliant and gifted academic who could rely on the solid German sociological tradition all while developing Dewey's pragmatism and Cooley's interactionism in a sociological vein. His interests included the dynamics of migration flows, the processes of settlement, and social inequalities (particularly within the American suburbs). His work, *The Polish Peasant in Europe and America* (Thomas and Znaniecki, 1918), a pioneering study developed with Florian Znaniecki about the communities of Polish peasants living in Illinois, was key influence in the development of the Department. Thomas' personality, his charisma, and peculiar approach to research offered a model of study that could bring together several techniques, methods, and disciplinary fields. Indeed, at the time the members of the School effectively introduced experiences and analytical methods that were typical of anthropology in the study of cities, complemented by a particular pragmatist-influenced focus on ethnography and social psychology. In this way, they combined a wide array of paradigms within one interpretive approach based on the relevance of large-scale empirical knowledge that has since emerged as one of the methodological tenets of the School; as a cornerstone of urban sociology practiced in Chicago. Until 1918, Thomas remained basically the driving force of the group of early researchers and was responsible for bringing the Department of Chicago to the forefront of the international scene with the influence obtained with his research. Finally, he should be credited for inviting to the School **Robert E. Park** (1864-1944), a key figure who would replace him as its leader after a few years, and who would lead the community of Chicago academics through what is unanimously defined as the golden age of the Chicago School.

The golden years: the city as laboratory

Robert Park came to Chicago with a highly prestigious academic background, having studied with John Dewey at the University of Michigan, with Georg Simmel in Berlin, and with William James in Harvard. He had also worked as an investigative reporter on the complex issues of blighted neighbourhoods in large cities such as Minneapolis, Detroit, and New York, and as a spokesman for Booker Washington, a prominent figure in the fight for the civil rights of African American citizens (Park, 1950; Matthews, 1977; Raushenbush, 1979). Park accepted Thomas' invitation and came to Chicago in 1914 for a first series of lectures that was followed by further studies and research. This activity earned him the respect and appreciation of his colleagues who had initially been wary of his not strictly academic approach. Yet, it was precisely his experience as a journalist and hands-on approach to the issues of urban life that led Park to become a key figure in the new and rich milieu of the School and the new approaches and scenarios produced over the next twenty years. Another quality Park had was his genuine ability to give cohesion to a research group that perhaps needed some motivation after Thomas had been forced to leave the Department due to differences with the University's management. Park's arrival also coincided with an all but complete decline of the reformist drive that in some ways had influenced the School's very first activities and its exponents Small and Thomas, who were close to the movements for social reform that had dominated the political debate in Chicago, at the time considered a paradigm of the modern city, a contemporary metropolis in full bloom.

A seminal text emerged in those years as the expression of the new direction of social research expressed by the group of Chicago researchers led by Park, at the centre of which was the need to understand modern society starting from our natural habitat: the city. *The City* (Park, 1915) appeared in 1915 in the American Journal of Sociology and reflected Cooley's ideas about the city as a social institution that could reveal the main traits of human nature as it was its direct expression: «Something more than a mere collective entity» (p. 3), the city is considered on the whole as an active process; not just a merely geographical aggregation but rather a constantly changing social organism created by the interaction between human beings and environment. In Park's words, the city had: «arisen in response to the needs of its inhabitants, once formed, impresses itself upon them as a crude external fact, and forms them, in turn, in accordance with the design and interests which it incorporates» (p. 4). This is one of the postulates of the Ecological School: the city is an environment *shaped* by human beings but it is crucially, in turn, capable of *shaping* them. In this regard, Park would write a few years later: «If the city is the world man has created, it is consequently the world he is condemned to live in. And so, indirectly and without a clear awareness of his own actions, man, in creating the city, has recreated himself» (Park, 1952, p. 72). In brief, for the Chicago school, ecological dynamics became the paradigm through which reading and translating the processes of evolution and transformation that take place in society were rendered into a scientific language.

Besides the issue of the city as the social habitat in which humans live in symbiosis and the organic concept of society as a system of shared symbolic meanings through which the human beings connect with each other, Park developed his first insights about the relationship between the communication media and the organization of democratic life by focusing in particular on the role of newspapers, the most powerful medium at the time, in shaping the social and industrial structures of the modern city (an issue he would later explore in a well-known study about the newspapers of immigrants' communities in America, *The Immigrant Press and Its Control* (1922)). Considered a classic also in the field of journalism studies, this text explores the role of the press as an institution that can provide the individual members of a community a common ground to nurture a new and lasting sense of belonging and identity by feeling part of one collective environment. On the other side, one of the lessons that Park, Small, and Thomas had learnt from German sociology and Simmel's teaching was precisely related to the need to give media a structuring function, in the sense that they had to facilitate the establishment of social relations within one specific horizon of possibilities offered by the ways media manifest themselves in daily life. In other words, media and institutions were studied in Chicago as agents of creation and stabilization of the social values in a community.

Finally, the 1915 article anticipated some of the School's theoretical-methodological foundations. First of all was the idea of considering the city «a social laboratory» (1915, p. 19) within which one should directly practice so-called participant observation as borrowed from the methods of ethnographic and anthropological research (Malinowski, 1922). Based on this approach, by actively participating in the social environment of concern to the particular study, the researcher performs a kind of research defined in qualitative terms precisely because it pursues a direct observation and collection of accounts, personal documents, life stories—just like Small, Thomas and the early group of pioneers of the School had done—that could contribute to an organic, coherent, and structured framework; a documentary method that mirrors large-scale empirical research models. In 1921, Park gave an organic form to his approach to research when he published a book that became a classic text of social sciences, *Introduction to the Science of Sociology* (Park and Burgess, 1921), co-authored with **Ernest W. Burgess** (1886-1966), who had studied with Small and was now his colleague. The book became a cornerstone for an entire generation of sociologists who studied in Chicago in those years, among many others: not coincidentally, the students on campus referred to it as "the Green Bible". Burgess' interests expanded the School's methodological horizon as they highlighted the processes of urban development, expansion, and the spatial relations established therein, therefore overcoming the canons of ethnographic analysis that focus instead on quantitative research methods. The reliance on schemes, maps, and spatial models within the ecological analysis also helped defining the traits of an actual methodological pluralism of urban geography. Open to new fields and mainly quantitative procedures, this foundation shortly inspired a large number of academics, including in particular **William Ogburn** (1886-1959): an academic who came to Chicago in 1927 after a period at Columbia University, and worked alongside Burgess as the main supporter of this approach.

Developments of human ecology

Besides the leading role of Park and Burgess, there are at least three other figures among the representatives of the Chicago School's golden years who are recognized for their contributions. The first one is **Ellsworth Faris** (1874-1953), an expert in social psychology and cultural anthropology, and director of the Department from 1925 to 1936. His presence helped the School keep alive a multiplicity of approaches and themes of interest by focusing its action on intercultural studies and therefore facilitating the interaction between the disciplines that had been the School's peculiar methodological approach from its outset. The second one is **Louis Wirth** (1897-1952) who had studied with Thomas and Park, and was an expert in immigration studies and the author of a text that greatly influenced the Chicagoan tradition. This book, *The Ghetto* (Wirth, 1928), is a cornerstone in the field of urban ethnography studies, the result of an in-depth investigation of the issues of intercultural integration in Chicago's immigrant communities, in particular the Jewish community in the early twentieth century. Given the large number—about one hundred—of ethnic groups living in Chicago, the city was a sort of ecological niche of unparalleled relevance for the experts who were then interested in finding empirical research models that could be applied on a larger scale to other major metropolitan contexts.

The third and last key figure of the time is **Roderick D. McKenzie** (1885-1940). Between 1923 and 1924 the Department began to receive substantial grants from the Laura Spellman Rockfeller Memorial (Kurtz, 1984, p. 62). For about ten years, such funding resulted in increased research activity and, as a consequence, in an increased publication of new studies. In 1925, McKenzie, who had studied with Park and Burgess, co-edited with them a collection of texts published under the title *The City* (Park, Burgess and McKenzie, 1925) that included some writings about the state of the art of the School. This volume is still considered the group's theoretical manifesto. For example, the book includes *The Natural History of the Newspaper* (p. 65), an essay by Park that carefully analyzes the role of the press and of newspapers as agents of human change that can influence the dynamics of social development and cultural interaction in an ecological perspective. The book also includes *The Growth of the City* (p. 49), an essay by Burgess that summarizes the meditations on the processes of urban development according to a spatial analysis. Based on this approach, the social structure of Chicago, a paragon of great expanding metropolises, is depicted as a series of concentric circles, a typical representation of urban space that since then has been called the Burgess Model. McKenzie contributed an essay titled *The Ecological Approach to the Study of the Human Community* (p. 59). This and other writings by the same author are included in a collection of texts published posthumously under the title *On Human Ecology* (McKenzie, 1968) that successfully and organically represents the convergence between urban planning and anthropology, social sciences and natural sciences in the frame of a methodological pluralism constantly pursued in the research activities developed by the members of the School (Hannerz, 1980, p. 105).

McKenzie's interpretive method is particularly useful to understand the approach later adopted by media ecology. In a wide-ranging and articulate manner, it shows the reliance on a biological metaphor, or the ecological paradigm through which the city and society on the whole should be considered as a living organism, based on the holistic model anticipated by pragmatism; an inseparable whole within which each component plays a particular role. The human community is viewed as the result of an ecological dynamic, the outcome of a competitive process, and the consequent adaptation that governs the spatial and temporal structure of society. Therefore, the city is a complex network of social relations; a dynamic and procedural system, the natural habitat of human development. Along these terms the concept of human ecology was anticipated a few years earlier in the field of chemistry by the American chemist Ellen Richards (1907) and in the field of biology by the Scottish biologist Patrick Geddes (1915; § 5.3). These scholars, who greatly influenced Lewis Mumford's research (§ 2.1), were also anticipated in the field of sociology by other thinkers such as Simmel, Toennies, Spencer, and Durkheim (Alihan, 1938; Shils, 1970; Hawley, 1950; 1971; 1989). Adopting the human ecology approach means observing the complexity of the symbiotic relationship between human beings and their environment with the awareness that behaviours, attitudes, and even the human processes of knowledge and feeling are deeply related to this social, cultural, and spatial environment. All things considered, this represents the most relevant heritage the intellectual tradition of media ecology received from the Chicago School. Seeing the media system as an actual environment within which humanity lives and acts ultimately means extending the relevance of human ecology, limited by the Chicagoans to the urban and social environment (the city as a medium) to the entirety of cultural expressive forms created by humans, thus the media in their widest meaning. In brief, these are viewed by media ecology as the expression of the human ecosystem that the Chicago School helped understand as a symbolic environment of social relationships.

Having reached these remarkable results in terms of both theoretical meditation and methodology and empirical research, the golden age of the Chicago School came to an end around the mid-thirties. Park retired from the University at the end of his academic career in 1933. The funding that had supported the activities of the group ceased and several lines and orientations of research began to emerge within the Department and made the overall frame of activities increasingly heterogeneous but in many ways weaker and more fragmented. During the 1940s, research and editorial activity continued with a diminished impetus compared to the previous decade. Soon after WWII, other members of the old guard such as Faris, Wirth, Burgess, and Ogburn also left the School. The relevance of the tradition established in Chicago in the golden years became increasingly weak, also due to the new and influential communities of sociological research that emerged in Los Angeles and Harvard campuses (Shils, 1970; Dear, 2002). But the original flame was not completely extinguished. In the 1950s and 1960s, a "second" Chicago School, recognized as such by the critics, began to emerge (Fine, 1995; Abbott 1999). In a less consolidated, although no less active form, different generations of academics pursued the same orientations and approaches developed during the golden age and anticipated a heritage that has been nurtured across the years and is still considered as a vibrant part of the conceptual and methodological background of American urban sociology (Thomas, 1983; Subtil, 2008). As such, the findings of the golden years of the Chicago school still exerts remarkable influence on the intellectual tradition of media ecology.

Chicago School thinkers' main works
The Organic Concept of Society (1895), Albion Small
Human Nature and the Social Order (1902), Charles Cooley
Social organization (1909), Charles Cooley
Introduction to the Science of Sociology (1921), R. Park, E. Burgess
The City (1925), Robert Park, Ernest Burgess, Roderick McKenzie
Mind, Self and Society (1934), George Mead
Human Communities. The City and Human Ecology (1952), Robert Park
On Human Ecology (1968), Roderick McKenzie

Further readings
Abbott A. (1999), *Department and Discipline. Chicago Sociology at One Hundred*, University of Chicago Press, Chicago.
Barnes S. (2002), "Media Ecology and Symbolic Interactionism", *Proceedings of the Media Ecology Association*, vol. 3, New York.
Blumer, H. (1969), *Symbolic interactionism. Perspective and method*, Prentice-Hall, Englewood Cliffs, N.J.
Burgess E.W., Bogue D.J., eds. (1964), *Contributions to Urban Sociology*, University of Chicago Press, Chicago.
Charon J.M. (1979), *Symbolic Interactionism. An introduction, an interpretation, an integration*, Prentice-Hall, Englewood Cliffs NJ.
Dear M., ed. (2002), *From Chicago to L.A. Making Sense of Urban Theory*, Sage, London.
Hannerz U. (1980), *Exploring the city. Inquiries toward an urban anthropology*, Columbia University Press, New York.
Hawley A. (1971), *Urban Society. An Ecological Approach*, Ronald Press, New York.
Hawley A. (1989), *Human Ecology. A Theoretical Essay*, University of Chicago Press, Chicago.
Harms W.F, DePencier I., eds.(1996), *Experiencing Education. 100 Years of Learning at The University of Chicago Laboratory Schools*, The University of Chicago Laboratory Schools, Chicago.
Harvey L. (1986), "The Myths of the Chicago School", *Quality and Quantity*, 20, 2-3, pp. 191-217.
Meltzer B.N., Peras J.W., Reynolds L.T., eds. (2014), *Symbolic Interactionism. Genesis, Varieties and Criticism*, Routledge, London.
Powell J.L. (2013), *Symbolic Interactionism, Nova Science*, New York.
Schubert H.J. (2006), "The Foundation of Pragmatic Sociology: Charles Horton Cooley and George Herbert Mead", *Journal of Classical Sociology*, 6, pp. 51-74.
Subtil F.B. (2008), *James Carey and the Legacy of Chicago School of Sociology on Communication and Media Studies*, International Sociological Association, Barcelona.
Thomas J. (1983), "The Chicago School. The Tradition and the Legacy", *Urban Quarterly*, 11, 4, pp. 387-511.

4.2 Gregory Bateson and the ecology of the mind

Exploring media ecology means observing the expressive forms of human culture, the dynamics of communication, and the development of the processes of perception and knowledge with the awareness that such issues distort a complex reality: the understanding of the deep interdependence between human beings and the environment. Within the intellectual tradition of media ecology, the very use of the word ecology becomes a sort of epistemological challenge that addresses once and for all the systemic nature of life in its entirety as a full interpenetration of humanity and the social, cultural, technological, as well as biological environment. There is one thinker in particular with whom media ecology is greatly indebted because of the utterly original perspective he proposed to observe the phenomena of the living world in all of its complexity. The impact of his intellectual development was such—sometimes with very different results—that he influenced an entire school, a movement of thought and a wide group of authors whose contribution was undeniably crucial for humanities in the late twentieth century. This thinker is Gregory Bateson (1904-1980), born in Britain but active in American academia, he was a forerunner of visual anthropology, the inspirer of the Palo Alto School, a pioneer of cybernetics, a symbol of American counter-culture and environmentalist movements, and an undisputed model for all the experts who, while studying human phenomena, approach an unusual and at the same time fascinating field created by this unique thinker: the ecology of the mind.

Born in Grantchester, a small city near Cambridge, the cradle of British philosophical and scientific research then dominated by men likes Russell and Whitehead, Bateson began his intellectual journey from a young age (Lipset, 1980; Lipset, 2009). His father was the biologist William Bateson, one of the founders of modern genetics. For his third son William Bateson had apparently imagined a career much like his own, particularly after losing his two first sons: one was killed during WWI and the other had taken his own life. After obtaining his degree in zoology with honors from Cambridge, Gregory started a career in academic research under his father's protective wing, a certainly cumbersome presence from whom he nonetheless inherited a unitary view of living forms by adopting an approach to the study of the biological world as a coherent network of systemic relations.

Wanting to break free from an already decided career as a biologist, the young Bateson found particular inspiration in anthropology. When his father died, in 1926, he decided to join an expedition to New Guinea. There, after years spent travelling for research, in 1931 he met Margaret Mead—the celebrated anthropologist with whom he started a first intellectual, then sentimental, relationship—whom he married five years later in Bali. During those years of research and study, another key figure of cultural anthropology, Ruth Benedict, became a fundamental influence on both Bateson and Mead. The results of the research conducted by Bateson in New Guinea were published under the title *Naven* (1936), an essay that for the first time presented descriptions and insights about the animist and totemist rituals of the Iatmul: a tribe of fishermen who lived along the central stretch of the Sepik river. The book, which was all but ignored by contemporary British anthropologists, has since been rehabilitated by modern anthropology. During some years in Bali, Bateson and Mead developed a form of anthropological research based on the production of video-photographic material and on the use of the most advanced recording techniques of the time; indeed, Bateson was a highly skilled photographer (Stagoll, 2009). The couple co-authored *Balinese Character. A Photographic Analysis* (Bateson and Mead, 1942), a text that, in many ways, pioneered the field of visual anthropology. After the expeditions in New Guinea and Bali—given the outbreak of WWII—Bateson worked as an anthropologist for the US Office of Strategic Services, first in Washington and, later, in US outposts in the South-Eastern Pacific. That emotionally troubling experience showed him the effects of putting the social sciences in the service of the goals of war.

The postwar period was a crucial turning point for Bateson, witnessing the celebrated Macy Conferences in New York: a series of cross-disciplinary meetings that triggered the birth of the cybernetics movement. Bateson and Mead were among the most brilliant voices of the group of academics—including Norbert Wiener, John von Neumann, Claude Shannon, Warren McCulloch—who contributed to the formative experience. The emergent paradigm of cybernetics and the radically innovative atmosphere of the Macy Conferences encouraged Bateson to integrate in one research approach an interest he had partly already explored that combined biological and social sciences, information theory and cognitive sciences, and to give them a unified meaning in line with the systemic view that cybernetic itself was effectively corroborating: a perspective later confirmed by the theory of general systems (Bertalanffy, 1969). However, there was no lack of conflicts within the group. The approach adopted by Bateson was criticized by those who viewed cybernetics as a technical discipline based on the study of models for the control of technological as well as information systems: prominent critics included Von Neumann, Weiner, and Shannon. Bateson nevertheless refused to reductively transfer these notions to human and social contexts and criticized the mechanistic and deterministic view taken by a large part of the group of detractors. He wanted, instead, to use cybernetics as an interpretive key of all the living systems in nature, therefore widening «the philosophical implications of cybernetics to the social and ecological fields» (Harries-Jones, 2009, p. 82). Although Bateson distanced himself from the positions that prevailed among the exponents of cybernetics, his ideas continued to greatly influence some members of the group, in particular the advocates of the so-called "second" cybernetics—Goffman (§ 4.2), Von Foester, Maturana, Varela—based on the study of biological, cognitive, and social systems.

In the meantime, Bateson had divorced Margaret Mead and, after a short and difficult period as a visiting professor in Harvard, finally moved to San Francisco due to the intervention of his friend, the anthropologist Alfred Kroeber. There, he began research in the field of psychiatry and psycho-therapy in 1949. As a contract professor at the California School of Fine Arts—currently the San Francisco Art Institute—and a consultant for the Veterans Administration Hospital in Palo Alto, he began to work specifically in psychiatry on substance use, family relations, deviant behaviour, and mental illness. In this context, Bateson developed his studies on human communication. A grant from the Rockefeller Foundation gave him the opportunity to establish a research group about these issues, the "Bateson project". The first group of researchers included Jay Haley, John Weakland, and Don Jackson. Over ten years, the group led by Bateson produced a remarkable amount of experimental research about schizophrenia and family therapy and developed what would be later known as the double bind theory. It was precisely an insistence on an emotional approach that Bateson had never fully approved of that over the years resulted in an irremediable rift with the other members of the group who, led by Don Jackson, in 1959 founded another centre to study systemic psycho-therapy, the Mental Research Institute in Palo Alto (Winkin, 1981; Sfez, 1990; Edmond and Picard, 2006) which was later brought to international attention by Paul Watzlawick and studies of the pragmatics of human communication (Watzlawick, Beavin and Jackson, 1967).

Dissatisfied with the progress of research in Palo Alto, in 1962 Bateson decided to leave California for the Virgin Islands and later for Hawaii for ethological study of play and animal communication, in particular among cetaceans. After about ten years, lack of funding forced Bateson to go back to California where he set about to publish *Steps to an Ecology of Mind* (1972), a collection of articles that illustrated the insights developed over more than twenty years of work in biology, anthropology, communication and psychology, and for the first time offered a comprehensive picture of his approach and method. The book was a breakthrough in Bateson's career. Over the ensuing years, it earned him several official acknowledgments, and in particular the appointment as a member of University of California's Board of Regents.

That said, the academic world still considered Bateson an awkward figure. Perhaps this element among others led him to embrace American counter-culture and concurrent ecological movements that were gaining attention on the international stage at the time. Although he sometimes criticized their ideological or pseudo-spiritual positions, he quickly became a true inspiration for those efforts, something of a guru of ecological thought. This was due to his unique charisma and remarkable gift as a speaker that partially reflected an innate inclination to the use of parables, tales, and metaphors as the elements of a method that constantly challenged reflexive thought; an explorative and dialogical approach condensed in his *metalogues*, the expressions of a contemporary maieutics developed as imaginary dialogues on the issues of knowledge.

In the late 1970s, although diagnosed with an incurable lung disease, Bateson, helped by Mary Catherine (his and Margaret Mead's daughter), published a new compendium of his thought aimed at a larger audience. *Mind and Nature* (1979) offered an original interpretation of the concept of mind viewed in its systemic nature as the expression of a convergence and a continuity between mental processes, human culture, and natural environment. His last work, *Angels Fear* (1987), was a collection of manuscripts that remained incomplete due to his death in 1980 but was posthumously completed by his daughter, Mary Catherine. Almost akin to the completion of an existential and spiritual path, the book deals with the theme of the sacred as the expression of an immanent holism between human culture and the natural environment, the reflection of the integrating dimension of human experience, but also a clear response to the detachment from the spiritual dimension of life in a society that was increasingly dominated by materialism and technology and unaware of an impending ecological upheaval on a global scale.

Systemic thought between mind and nature

From this biographical background Gregory Bateson emerges as a wandering, fleeting thinker who would seem not to fit into any particular intellectual or academic category. A troubled path, marked by death—one brother killed in war, another who took his own life—three marriages, intellectual arguments, and financial hardship, certainly contributed to the rich personal and scientific figure of a man who transcended his own time and was defined by his biographer as an "anachronistic" thinker (Lipset, 1980, p. XII). Beyond the clichés with which his thought is often associated today—the guru of American counter-culture, the prophet of environmentalism, the cult figure of Californian new age—what remains are the traces of an accidental, random, creative process that led Bateson to become a key figure of systemic thinking due to his nomadic approach to knowledge. By moving with nonchalance between natural and philosophical science and refusing to attach himself to one discipline in particular, and never obtaining a permanent academic position, Bateson worked with a truly scientific conviction and explored always original and never obvious paths. By transcending the very idea of interdisciplinarity, he rather pursued the similarities between different disciplines in an effort to define an organic view of the living world, an ecological awareness in order to explore «the systemic nature of the human beings, the systemic nature of the culture in which they lives, and the systemic nature of the biological, ecological system around them» (Bateson, 1972, p. 474).

Given the remarkable amount of insights in Bateson's work, and the risk of limiting the richness of his thought to a restricted number of notions or definitions, it is difficult to isolate the continuity with—and elements it has imparted to—the intellectual tradition of media ecology. Rather than rushing to certainly partial if not temporary conclusions, it might be more useful to isolate at least the methodological foundations, the preliminary insights and conceptual tenets that would help determine, if not an actual heritage, at least a fundamental epistemology that Bateson's thought shares with media ecology.

A first preliminary insight and fundamental conceptual assumption of Bateson's method is his awareness of the obsolescence of some historical-philosophical tenets—in particular, the expression of a "one-sided progress" (Bateson, 1979, p. 288)—firmly rooted in modern thinking, articulated first of all in a rigid mind/matter opposition reflecting the dualism advanced by Descartes (p. 285) and a host of other dualisms (emotion/reason, organism/environment, individual/society, nature/culture) embedded in the development of Western philosophy. Bateson countered this view which mirrored the mechanistic models typical of a certain analytic thought of positivistic nature with an idea of "mind" defined by a holistic view of the mental process, a system within which the organism cannot be separated from its environment and there is, therefore, no room for the famous distinction between *res cogitans* and *res extensa*. By challenging apparent reductionism and dualism in Western thought, Bateson ultimately inaugurated a new ecological awareness of the relationship of organism and environment conceived as an organic entity, a system of related elements based on a holistic view of the world as defined by his famous phrase, «*the pattern which connects*» (Bateson, 1979, p. 21). For this reason, the "mind" is an ecology and Bateson views it as an entity that connects complementary systemic processes such as human culture and our biological environment. According to this approach, developed by Bateson from insights resulting from the paradigm of cybernetics and the systems theory (Bateson, 1972, p. 363)—similar to the pragmatic stance of C.S. Peirce who had postulated the concept of *synechism* as a kind of continuity between mind and nature (Peirce, 1931-35)—the very idea of mind transcends the boundary of the individual, subsumes a multiplicity of parts, and expands into the aspects of human action that work systemically such as a culture, a language, and a form of knowledge.

In the ecology of the mind proposed by Bateson, all the expressive forms of human culture create a network, interacting with each other, and thus interconnecting to establish a coherent, systemic, and consistent multiplicity that is in a certain sense alive because it is inherently connected with the development of the living entity that is the natural environment. Media themselves are elements of the *pattern which connects*, an integral feature of the ecology of the mind (and, similarly, one of media ecology's main insights) and not just tools, and thus as such external, separate, and independent. In other words, media are viewed as part of a systemic context within which humans live. They are elements of the systemic network that includes both human beings and the environment. Therefore, according to the ecology of the mind, every environment, including the media environment, is considered in a broad sense «not as a fixed factor that is separate from the organism but as an interdependent variable, modified by and at the same time capable of modifying the organism» (Strate, 2013, p. 205). Viewing media in ecological terms means recognizing the deep relation between human beings and what surrounds them, between our way of thinking and our way of living: in other terms, it means recognizing the isomorphism between biological evolution and mental processes. The co-evolutionary nature of the ecology of the mind also implies a systemic view, and frames the conceptual couples nature/culture, technology/society, individual/environment—unshakeable foundations of the modern philosophical tradition influenced by dualistic thought—in a monism in order to observe another key element of the living systems: the complexity of the relational connections inherent in communication processes.

The Palo Alto School and the 'invisible college'

Communication is a central issue of the second methodological premise media ecology inherits from Gregory Bateson. The exchange and sometimes the intellectual conflicts with the pioneers of cybernetics and the experimentation on psychological dynamics in family contexts developed by Bateson during his long experience in Palo Alto certainly helped him build a vision of communication as a dynamic, relational, contextual, or ecological process. Consistent with the organicist turning point Bateson had experienced in those years, such a vision triggered a major impact on a wide range of academics from different disciplinary fields who were variously interested in the processes of communication and were ready to embrace a substantially new interpretive paradigm, an alternative to the linear model of communication followed by cybernetics experts of the mathematical-informational kin. In order to define the impact of this interpretive turning point, some have argued for the existence of if not an actual School, at least of a sort of "invisible college" (Winkin, 1981) in which the members included a substantial group of thinkers who shared the systemic and relational approach at the core of Bateson's ecology of the mind. These included, first and foremost, **Don Jackson** (1920-1968) and **Paul Watzlawick** (1921-2007), who worked at the Palo Alto Mental Research Institute in the field of psychiatry. Along with Janet Beavin, both advocated the *Pragmatics of human communication* (Watzlawick, Beavin and Jackson, 1967) that basically resulted from Bateson's theories about the double bind as well as from a circular, relational, and contextual idea of communication. As supporters of a strictly behavioural perspective, the members of the Palo Alto Mental Research Institute started a fruitful research endeavour in the field of psychotherapy; one aimed at understanding the deepest effects of communication on human behaviour. Such an approach, encapsulated in the five well-known "axioms of communication" (pp. 40-61), highlights the relational, contextual, and environmental models that result from communication processes. These may be subsumed in the idea of meta-communication (p. 43)—another concept borrowed from Bateson's thought—which, in the authors' words, is «communication about communication» (p. 45), or the system of more or less explicit information components that can influence the content of any communication interaction (Winkin, 1981; Porcar and Hainic, 2011; Strate, 2013).

Two remarkable academic figures related to the invisible college in Palo Alto applied this same line of thought to anthropology. **Ray Birdwhistell** (1918-1994), for example, had studied in Chicago under George Mead (§ 4.1) and was connected with several members of the Toronto School (§ 3). He also contributed to the Macy Conferences in New York and collaborated with Margaret Mead and Bateson in Bali. Birdwhistell is considered one of the pioneers of *kinesics* (Birdwhistell, 1952), a peculiar field of anthropological research and communication that generally analyzes human gestures related to the use of language and the context within which they occur (1970). In his studies, verbal and non-verbal communication are viewed as part of the same "transactional" system (Birdwhistell, 1952, p. 104), or a multi-faceted and multi-sensorial system of interaction based on which body messages, gestures and language are all to be considered in their overall meaning, all while acknowledging their relational complexity (Ekman, 1985).

The second prominent academic who can be variously related to the Palo Alto School is **Edward T. Hall** (§ 4.3), an anthropologist and linguist who was equally influenced by the Chicago School's ecological approach (§ 4.1) and was connected with some members of the Toronto School (§ 3). He was also close to the so-called linguistic relativism advocated by Edward Sapir and Benjamin Whorf, and to the cultural relativism (§ 4.3) inspired by the research conducted by Margaret Mead and Ruth Benedict in the vein of Franz Boas' school and teaching. A pioneer of intercultural communication studies (Hall, 1959; Rogers et al., 2002), and a trail-blazer in the fields of *proxemics* (Hall, 1966) (the study of human spatial requirements in interpersonal and social communication) and *chronemics* (1983) (the study of how time is perceived and used in communication), Hall conceptualized communicative action as a complex territorial, or spatial, based relational system. Therefore, communication is an experiential process that constantly occurs through and is more or less openly influenced by an environment, a territory, a place, a cultural and social space that corresponds to the "hidden dimension" (1966) of communication clearly related to Bateson's systemic, holistic, connective and organicist paradigm.

Finally, a third prominent academic who may be included in the so-called invisible college of Palo Alto is **Erving Goffman** (1922-1982), a Canadian sociologist who also frequently contributed to the Macy Conferences and was connected to the work group led by Bateson in the late 1950s. Goffman had studied in Toronto with Charles Hart and Ray Birdwhistell and followed the scholarship of symbolic interactionism founded by Charles Cooley and George Mead at the Chicago School (§ 4.1) as well as the European sociological tradition developed by Durkheim and Simmel (Burns, 1992; Winkin and Leeds-Hurwitz, 2013). Goffman thought that every communication interaction occurs within a social space or situation (Meyrowitz, 1985, p. 37), or a system of possible behavioural configurations that influence individual actions at a symbolic level. He argued this approach through a successful dramatic analogy as hinted by the title of one of his most famous work, *The Presentation of Self in Everyday Life* (Goffman, 1959). Daily relational habits and communication exchanges are interpreted in an analogy with the dynamics of theatre presentation where masks, roles, and behaviours are the result of more or less explicit conditionings determined by what happens on the stage or in the backstage of any social situation within which an individual acts. In other words, the behavioural dynamics of any communication interaction is influenced by actual social rituals (1967) that Goffman would later define as contextual and environmental *frames* (1974) within which the experience of communication occurs.

Meta-communication and relational contexts

The approaches adopted by Jackson, Watzlawick, Birdwhistell, Hall, Goffman—mostly rooted in Bateson's thinking—share an almost obvious assumption: communication processes always occur within a relational systems. Rather than separate, communication processes are fully part of the wider ecology of the mind described by Bateson as a direct expression of the systemic nature of any living environment. Starting from the assumptions of information theory as it had been illustrated by the champions of cybernetics (Shannon and Weaver, 1949), and at the same time trying to overcome the mechanistic and technical aspects that prevented its application to human and social contexts, Bateson considered the concept of *difference* in his meditation on the relational nature of communication.

His definition of information as «a difference which makes a difference» (Bateson, 1972, p. 364) is universally known. In his attempt to amend the postulates of cybernetics and apply the theory of logical types formulated by Russel and Whitehead to the human and social sciences, Bateson adopted the conceptual class of change and reformulated it in order to observe the processes of communication in an ecological perspective. According to this approach, information occurs whenever there is a change, a transformation, a difference in a systemic configuration. During his experience in New Guinea, Bateson had already used the conceptual class of difference as a typical element for the interpretation of the interactions within a culture, and for that purpose he had created the concept of *schismogenesis* (Bateson, 1936). In a wider perspective, any change occurring in the relational balance of a living system has a semantic value. In other words, Bateson overcame the reductionism of the sender-channel-receiver model and proposed communication as a relational phenomenon between organisms rather than a transfer of information, where the "difference" lies precisely in the relational changes related to a wider systemic context that places them in another, more elevated, comprehensive, and transversal horizon of meaning. This is actually a *meta*—from the Greek "beyond" or "after"—level of communication, the systemic environment within which the communication processes occur according to a relational logic. In Bateson's own words: «it is the *context* that fixes the meaning» (Bateson, 1979, p. 31), or there is a *meta-communication*—a concept that was later explicitly appropriated by the Palo Alto group (Watzlawick, Beavin and Jackson, 1967)—that underlies the relation between the subjects who participate in a communication interaction. In addition, and accordingly with the perspective of Gestalt psychology, Bateson introduced the idea of contextual frames of behaviour (1972, p. 197), or meta-communication frames. This concept was later expressly by Goffman (Goffman, 1974) as a system of unconscious mind habits; for example non-verbal or para-verbal kinds of communication – that in a certain context trigger causality models at a much more complex level than behavioural psychology had tried to explain. In short, Bateson argued that communication should be viewed as a contextual frame, the texture, the connecting pattern, or a "meta-structure" (1979, p. 25) that influences the development of relational processes, once more according to a systemic, environmental, and ultimately ecological logic: an actual ecology of communication.

All of the above has a crucial impact on media ecology. Any form of human expression, first of all language and with it play, art, rituals, or the fields of human creativity dominated by the symbolic dimension of communication interaction, contribute to an ecological context, a meta-structure, an environment that surrounds the way of thinking, feeling, acting, and particularly interacting. Therefore, *context*, a key word in Bateson's lexicon (1979, p. 30), acquires a particularly relevant role for the understanding of human expressive forms—the media in their widest meaning—including the information processes. According to Bateson, any gesture or thought, just like any interpretation of meaning, is closely related to its surroundings or environment, or to the context within which it occurs. Otherwise said, the question is acknowledging the particular primacy of the relationship. As Bateson wrote: «the relationship comes first, it *precedes*» (Bateson, 1979, p. 179).

In the ecology of the mind, everything is interconnected and interrelated. Therefore, the expressive forms of human culture can be observed under a new light in terms of relationship. As a manifestation of the ecology of the mind, or an expression of a living system that exceeds, and basically incorporates, the human organism, media are an environment, a context, a frame—or in Bateson's terms, a relational ecology. They establish a pattern that connects the multiplicity of human experience without necessarily having a causal-deterministic connection with it, or a univocal influence between context and element. There is instead a system, a relationship of mutual interpenetration.

This is basically the second and perhaps the most important intellectual insight media ecology inherited from Gregory Bateson. As the pioneer of an actual "systemic wisdom" (Stagol, 2009, p. 50), an activist of "philosophical practice" (Rovatti, 2009, p. 9), Bateson initiated a new way of conceiving human processes. The holistic and contextual perspective of the ecology of the mind brings every meditation back to human nature, or to the way human beings feel, think and act, to a principle of awareness; the awareness of belonging to wider cultural, social, and natural systems of which the media, the expressive forms of human culture, are a direct expression.

Gregory Bateson's main works
Naven (1936)
Balinese Character. A Photographic Analysis (1942), with M. Mead
Communication: The Social Matrix of Psychiatry (1951), with J. Ruesch
Steps to an Ecology of Mind (1972)
Mind and Nature (1979)
Angels Fear (1987), with Mary Catherine Bateson

Further readings
Brockman J., ed. (1977), *About Bateson. Essays on Gregory Bateson*, Dutton, New York.
Chaney A. (2017), *Runaway. Gregory Bateson, the double bind, and the rise of ecological consciousness*, University of North Carolina Press, Chapel Hill.
Charlton N.G. (2008), *Understanding Gregory Bateson. Mind, beauty, and the sacred earth*, State University of New York Press, Albany NY.
Harries-Jones P. (1995), *A Recursive Vision. Ecological Understanding and Gregory Bateson*, University of Toronto Pres, Toronto.
Lipset D. (1980), *Gregory Bateson. The Legacy of a Scientist*, Beacon Press, Boston.
Rieber R.W., ed. (1989), *The Individual, communication, and society. Essays in memory of Gregory Bateson*, Cambridge University Press, New York.
Steier F., Jorgenson J., eds. (2005), *Gregory Bateson: Essays for an Ecology*

of Ideas, special issue, Cybernetics & Human Knowing, 12, 1-2.
Strate L. (2013), "Gregory Bateson and Paul Watzlawick. From the Ecology of Mind to the Pragmatics of Media Ecology", *Explorations in Media Ecology*, 12, 3-4, pp. 199-207.
Watzlawick P., Beavin B. J., Jackson D.D. (1967), *Pragmatic of human communication. A study of interactional patterns, pathologies, and paradoxes*, Norton, New York.

Documentary films
An Ecology of Mind (2010), Nora Bateson

4.3 Edward Hall and cultural ecology

The cross-disciplinary nature of media ecology can be particularly recognized in a vitally important issue, a vibrant testing ground constantly addressed by the twentieth-century tradition that reveals a transversal, fascinating, and at the same time complex element in its very roots. This issue is culture—an age-old but everlasting key theme that, perhaps for its inherent critical value, has attracted the interest of countless academics and has stimulated philosophical as well as historical, economical, and sociological research, and has ultimately become the main axis of a vast and fruitful disciplinary field—cultural anthropology. A key figure of media ecology's intellectual tradition can be related precisely with the meditation on the concept of culture that, since the very first definition of culture formulated in anthropology in 1871 by Edward Burnett Tylor (1871), has nurtured a remarkable part of anthropological research. This figure is Edward T. Hall (1914-2009) who was briefly discussed earlier for his intellectual relationship with some members of the Palo Alto School (§ 4.2) and the research group that grew around the journal *Explorations* under the leadership of Carpenter and McLuhan in Toronto during the 1950s (§ 3).

Born in Webster Groves, a town near St. Louis, Missouri, Hall was working in the construction industry in the early 1920s when he discovered the Hopi and Navajo native reservations in Arizona and so developed an interest for human ethnic groups and their cultural diversity (Hall 1992). He studied cultural and social anthropology at Columbia University, the main academic centre for anthropology at the time. During WWII, Hall served with the US troops in Europe, Africa, and the Philippines and experienced first-hand the key issue of ideological-cultural conflicts of the global war. Between 1951 and 1955, he started an academic career alongside key anthropology experts such as Ruth Benedict, Ralph Linton, Abram Kardiner, Clyde Kluckhohn and he continued his intense research activity with the US government as an anthropologist with the Foreign Service Institute, a State Department agency that managed diplomatic relationships and foreign affairs for postwar reconstruction in occupied territories (Hall, 1992; Leeds-Hurwitz, 1990; Rogers et al., 2002). In the following years he continued to work as a researcher and teacher and contributed to several high-profile academic institutions—in Vermont his colleague Erich Fromm advised him to study Freud, for instance—with a remarkable and unceasing publishing activity of essays on cultural anthropology, linguistics, animal behaviour, and psycho-analysis.

Hall's intellectual development was particularly influenced by **Franz Boas** (1858-1942), a German academic who had studied physics and geography before moving to the US where he became an undisputed pioneer of anthropology and helped overturn the then-prominent late nineteenth-century evolutionist and ethnocentric approach. His research promoted an actual turning point for anthropology as it considered every culture in its own specificity and refused to establish a hierarchy based on evolutionary reasons. This new approach originated what is somewhat doubtfully considered as the so-called Boas school with a following that included key exponents of American cultural anthropology, linguistics, and ethnographic research such as Edward Sapir, Ruth Benedict, Margaret Mead, Benjamin Whorf. The Freudian psycho-analytic paradigm on one side, and the anthropological tradition established by Boas on the other inspired Hall to build a robust theoretical and methodological approach based on the deep connection between the two pillars of his thinking—culture and communication processes—both contributing to the idea of intercultural communication, a field of study he undisputedly pioneered (Winkin, 1981; Bennet, 1998; Rogers et al., 2002).

The worlds of relativism

Hall's meditation on intercultural communication, developed through empirical research conducted at the Foreign Service Institute alongside the linguist George Trager—who had studied with Sapir and Whorf—and the anthropologist Ray Birdwhistell—who had studied with George Mead in Chicago—starts with *The Silent Language* (Hall, 1959). The book, the first of his best-known works—and an unexpected success translated into several languages that would also make him quite popular—highlights some meaningful features in Hall's thinking from which media ecology derived several insights. The title clearly evokes the hidden elements underlying interpersonal relationships, or the nonverbal elements of human communication that Hall began to research in an original attempt based on the ethnographic work he had developed in the native reservations in Arizona that he later called *proxemics* (1966), or the study of space management and the effect of distances on interpersonal communication which was complemented by research on gestures developed by Birdwhistell (1952) about *kinesics*, later expanded to the study of the cultural views of time through the notion of *chronemics* (Hall, 1983). The relevance of the ethnographic and anthropological approach in the method Hall adopted to understand communication processes can be measured through the focus on culture constantly recognizable in the book. Its main subject is indeed the function of communication *within*, as well as *between* each different culture, starting from the pluralistic acknowledgment of their basic differences and individual peculiarity. This implies an explicit support of the paradigm of so-called *linguistic relativism*, a very productive current of North American cultural anthropology that deeply influenced twentieth-century philosophical discourse, although it was cautiously received particularly by European critics (Borowsky, 2000).

The methodological foundation of linguistic relativism, or the principle of linguistic relativity, is that language's function is not simply to describe the world and reality surrounding us. Language, instead, shapes or at least influences our way of thinking or our way of perceiving reality and experiencing the world (Lyons, 1981). The canonical expression of this speculative approach is rooted in meditations about the nature of languages— in other terms, linguistic perspectivism—particularly in the work of the German philosopher Wilhelm von Humboldt (1820) and Durkheim (1895) about categories of thought and in Boas' ethnographic research (1911) on American First Nations. Actually, a somewhat standard version of linguistic relativism may be traced back to the studies conducted by **Edward Sapir** (1884-1939), a student of Boas also of German origin, who worked between Canada and the US, in the universities of Yale and Chicago in close contact with the members of the Chicago School (§ 4.1). In his classic text *Language* (1921), Sapir introduces an approach to the understanding of language that reflects both Freudian psycho-analytic influences and Boas' approach in the sense that, due to the connection between thinking and language, the latter is viewed in its psychic and individual dimension as well as in the collective dimension as "historical product" (Sapir, 1921, p. 148) that effectively works as an instrument of psychological-cultural identification and as a leading factor of social reality. Sapir also sensed the revolutionary relevance of the still emerging remote communication technologies—starting with the radio—and actually anticipated some insights on contemporary neo-tribalism that was argued by some exponents of the Toronto School a few years later (§ 3). Research conducted later by Sapir's best-known student, **Benjamin Lee Whorf** (1897-1941), should be considered equally relevant as it formalized the studies about the relationship between language and culture. Whorf was a chemical engineer by profession who, after meeting Sapir in Yale in 1928, decided to focus on a comparative study of First Nations languages and cultures that effectively inaugurated the current of comparative linguistics (Nystrom, 2006, p. 285). By developing the insights in Sapir's works, he formalized the principle of linguistic relativity (Whorf, 1959), a theory now indissolubly tied to his name.

Although the studies conducted by Sapir and Whorf have been generally known since the 1950s as the "Sapir-Whorf hypothesis", or Whorfianism, this definition has raised some doubts because they never actually authored a joint publication on the subject. Despite this, the convergence of their research attracted a remarkable interest ever since, and not merely from anthropologists or linguists. Within media ecology, for example, this approach would be adopted with particular adjustments by Neil Postman and Charles Weingartner (§ 2.3) among others. The so-called Sapir-Whorf hypothesis argues that every language shapes a particular perception of reality and organizes forms of experience as the interpenetration between subject and object of perception, between human beings and the environment. This approach also mirrors the anti-positivist attitude that led to the birth of the era of so-called pragmatism in North America and promoted most insights of the so-called Boas School and the Chicago School (§ 4.1), including the interactionist current and more in general the emerging tradition of media ecology itself. Every language, based on its specific cultural domain, is viewed as an element with a certain degree of autonomy that can generate a particular form of experience, a certain vision of the world in its users. In other words, this approach argues that each culture lives in and is reflected by language. In this regard, the German philosopher Hans-Georg Gadamer proposed an even more radical interpretation: «Language speaks us, rather than we speak it» (Gadamer, 1969, p. 529). Ultimately, here is an equally radical synthesis: more than describing the world, language creates it. According to Whorf (1956), every language influences the thought and therefore human behaviour promotes observations and assessments of reality that are directly connected to and therefore determined by that linguistic system: hence, the definition of this approach as *linguistic determinism*. In other words, languages define «both how the individuals that speak them conceptualize the reality that surrounds them and how they perceive» (Lyons, 1981, p. 312). But every language is the expression of a particular cultural configuration; it organizes reality according to specific categories in relation with different conceptual systems on a structural and functional level therefore relative to the culture that generated them (p. 18): hence the idea of relativism.

Hall's belief in linguistic relativism/determinism led him to further research communication processes inspired by anthropological research conducted by Sapir and Whorf in line with Boas' tradition. Hall realized that the principles defined in relation with the study of languages and interpersonal communication could be applied with equally good results to the study of human behaviour in general, or to the entirety of culture. The relevance of this approach is concisely expressed as follows: «culture is communication and communication is culture» (1959, p. 243). This means that each culture in its specificity has a special formative power, the power to influence the communication experience, based precisely on those cultural behaviours; the invisible and silent elements in the non-verbal and gestural forms of communication or in the management of space and distances that implicitly and almost unconsciously guide any kind of interaction. Obviously, Hall considers the expressive forms of communication as an unconditional reflection of the culture that generated them. By following Freud's argument, he conceived of a cultural unconscious, a hidden code that operates simultaneously at different levels of conscience within that expression of the human symbolic system that is communication. In other words, culture and communication are inseparable and our various cultural behaviours are ultimately communication systems that human beings develop within various groups on a range that is remarkably wider than the limited one we commonly use to describe the narrowly-defined phenomena of communication as such. In short, from a strictly ecological perspective, culture may be viewed as a structured system of codes that establishes a symbolic space of human interaction, an environment within which communication occurs. And, as such, the environment influences and shapes communication and culture reciprocally and generates meaning that can always be traced back to the environment. Each communicative interaction uses culture as an environment, a medium, a place. Therefore, according to Hall's approach, culture *is* a medium, an environment, a territory that systematically influences the dynamics of each communication interaction. In even clearer terms, the concept of culture as communication expressed by Hall means that it is culture, with its own linguistic code, that communicates; *with* itself and *for* itself, through the individuals that are part of it. All of these positions basically describe a kind of ecology of communication.

When Hall pushed his meditations on linguistic determinism a little bit further, and therefore contemplated all the material or ideational factors that contribute to the specific features of a certain culture within a systemic and integrated logic, he actually simply embraced an equally fruitful current in American anthropology, *cultural relativism*. The relativistic approach that can be recognized in Boas and in his followers may be indeed applied not just to the linguistic factors that, as seen above, shape every cultural domain by organizing forms of experience. From a psycho-analytic perspective, this approach is also extremely useful to explain all the factors that shape human experience in aspects of social, religious, ethical, and aesthetical organization. The idea of culture that emerges from cultural relativism can guide human behaviours, shape beliefs, assessments, categories of thought, and therefore any aspect of individual life within that culture. In other words, we can recognize the connection between cultural and psychological processes that contribute to shape individual identity. In this regard, it is important to mention another theoretical current commonly known as Culture and Personality School that, although with several approaches and solutions, embraced the remarkable influence of the idea of culture and its reciprocal influence on the individual and explain the individual reactions to such influence through neuropsychology and psycho-analysis (Borowsky, 1994; Cuche, 2004). Simultaneously supporting the Boas paradigm and the anthropological results of the psycho-analytical approach, Hall remained basically aligned to this current that was also advocated by some prominent figures in his academic training, including Benedict and in particular Linton and Kardiner.

Humanity and our extensions

In a later work, *The Hidden Dimension* (1966), Hall's arguments about the communication aspects of cultural behaviours are extended well beyond the area of interpersonal and social interaction. By approaching the study of culture in its entirety, Hall provides some remarkably relevant theoretical advancements that make anthropological knowledge particularly important for the intellectual tradition of media ecology. The first of such concerns the focus on space and time within the processes that shape every culture. Proxemics and chronemics—defined by Hall while offering a specific taxonomy (1966, p. 143; 1983, p. 13)—are two concepts that are not simply related to the relational and communication dynamics recognizable, although with remarkable differences, in every culture. Hall considers them as distinctive features, therefore as the reflection of a specific cultural configuration that can shape the forms of experience in the individuals that are part of that culture, thus providing varying and peculiar views of the world. Therefore, the ways of conceiving space and time can be conceived as a sort of cultural *a priori* and represent the invisible background that shapes a culture and at the same time makes it different from all the others. The central role of space and time in Hall's view puts him in direct connection with the interpretive line proposed by Harold Innis (§ 2.1; Flayhan, 2002, p. 9) that recognizes the distinctive role played by these two elements in the forms of production, preservation, and propagation of knowledge in the different ages of human culture in an historical, economical, and political perspectives.

The second theoretical tenet that emerges from the research conducted by Hall on culture seems in line with both the interactionist approach proposed by the Chicago School (§ 4.1) and the psycho-analytical approach of the Culture and Personality School that Hall relied on to develop his own speculative system. Every symbolic system humans live in, every culture in its own way, promotes specific experience-shaping processes, and therefore contributes to the construction of constantly original perceptive universes. As a result, structures of experience are shaped by culture. Hall writes: «Experience is something man projects on the outside world as he gains it in its culturally determined form » (1959, p. 244). Based on this assessment, the entirety of culture deeply influences the use of the senses, or the perceptive interface through which human beings experience the outside world. The entire aesthetical apparatus is shaped by culture as a kind of sensorial background, a perceptive world, the foundation of habits, models of behaviour, ways of perceiving and conceptualizing reality, or the very forms of human experiences, (Hall, 1966, p. 129). Hall sees this as a kind of *sensory relativism*, as «people who grew in different cultures also live in different sensory worlds» (p. 225). This argumentative approach somehow evokes the ideas developed by Walter Ong (§ 3.3), who articulated a well-defined periodization of the great human anthropological cycles—primary orality, literacy and secondary orality—precisely in the light of the requirements of adjusting and balancing human sensory components induced by the different communication forms cyclically emerging in a certain culture or historical age.

The third insight provided by Hall that would become an exceptionally relevant element within the debate on the nature of media and more in general within the vast continent of philosophy of technology is the idea of considering the entirety of cultural artifacts as actual prostheses or extensions of human abilities. In this regard, Hall uses the word *extensions* that became a commonly invoked metaphor in media ecology (Flayhan, 2002). Hall writes: «The study of man is a study of his extensions» (Hall, 1976, p. 38). Any human artifact—whether material or ideological; any technology, instrument, invention—should be considered as an extension of humanity; or an extension of our physical, psychic, and sensory abilities. All of these extensions create a network of support through which humans interact with the world by modifying it, and shaping it based on our own needs and requirements. Hall explains: «Today man has developed extensions for practically everything he used to do with his body. [...] In fact, all man-made material things can be treated as extensions of what man once did with his body or some specialized part of his body» (1959, p. 26). Therefore, every extension plays a particular mediating role; or *mediates* the relationship between human beings and the environment. «The territory,» Hall argues, «is in every sense of the word an extension of the organism, which is marked by visual, vocal and olfactory signs. Man has created material extensions of territoriality as well as visible and invisible territorial markers» (1966, p. 131).

The idea of culture that emerges from Hall's ideas is that of a primary, if not exclusive, feature of the human condition. It is rooted in humanity's ability to interact with our environment by transforming it over time through the layering of the extensions or ourselves we acquire and convey socially. Therefore, Hall's view is in agreement with a broader current of cultural anthropology that considers culture as the sum of features of human condition socially rather than genetically or biologically inherited. This is not so distant from the canonical definition of culture proposed in 1871 by Edward B. Tylor, one of the pioneers of anthropology: «that complex whole [...] of capabilities and habits acquired by man as a member of society» (Tylor, 1871, p. 1). In addition, Hall develops his concept of culture from a strictly ecological perspective, or the idea that culture itself results from the special connection between human beings and our environment. He writes: «the relationship of man to his extensions is simply a continuation and a specialized form of the relationship of organisms in general to their environment» (Hall, 1966, p. 234). Therefore, culture is naturally connected with humanity's ability to extend itself in our environment by forming new and different environments that, as such, acquire the features of the culture that generated them in an autopoietic process. In other words, «as man developed culture he domesticated himself and in the process created a whole new series of worlds, each different from the other» (Hall, 1966, pp. 12-13).

Finally, according to Hall, if on one side of society extends itself through its cultural artifacts in order to shape it according to its needs and models of thought, on the other side, once these extensions have propagated around it, they act as environmental, sometimes invisible, forces, that establish a new environment in turn capable of stimulating new cultural attitudes and ways of approaching reality. The ultimate assumption is that «Man has created a new dimension, the cultural dimension» (Hall, 1966, p. 11), and in this new dimension we live, act, think, ultimately build our own vision of the world. But this dimension—the word in question evoking a territorial, spatial, environmental analogy without coincidence—is in many ways hidden and invisible due to humanity's incomplete awareness of the cultural unconscious that, as explained by the anthropological tradition influenced by Freud, we are forced to deal with. It affects, influences and, in a more radical sense, imposes a certain perception of the world: «Man cannot divest himself of his own culture», as Hall argues (1966, p. 234). In other words, this is a feedback effect, a rebound, a retroactive process: humans transform their environment but at the same time they are transformed by it, sometimes in an unconscious way.

Hall's vision—his interpretation of culture in light of the relationship between humanity, extensions of ourselves, and our environment—attracted a remarkable interest in the Toronto research group led by Carpenter and McLuhan. The latter, in particular, adopted the concept of extensions (in place of the terms *uttering* and *outering* as had been formerly employed) in part borrowed from Hall's work (McLuhan, 1962, p. 26). As documented in a considerable volume of correspondence, the two scholars established an intellectual partnership, facilitated by Carpenter himself, in the late 1950s (Molinaro et al., 1987; Rogers, 2000). This partnership, based on the shared advocacy of the concept of extensions—that McLuhan would actually also attribute to Buckminster Fuller (1938; Rogers, 2000, p. 122)—led McLuhan to describe media precisely as "extensions of man"; a phrase later used as the subtitle and argumentative background of his best-known work, *Understanding Media* (McLuhan, 1964a).

Beyond materialism

A further consideration should be made about Hall's relationship with another important current of North American cultural anthropology. His focus on complex of cultural artifacts as an element that can reveal the primary features of a certain culture is such that his approach can be related to the current of *cultural materialism* mainly advocated by **Marvin Harris** (1927-2001). Harris also came from the intellectual environment of Columbia University and had long worked as an ethnographic researcher in the native cultures of Latin America. He then basically abandoned the then-prevalent Boas-influenced approach and, starting from a materialistic approach to history largely inspired by Marx and Engels (although lacking their dialectical character), he directed his research towards forms of material culture which he conceived as guiding elements of the processes of cultural transformation and evolution. Harris tried to combine two positions that at the time appeared to provide an alternative to the psycho-analytical paradigm influenced by Boas on one hand and to the Marxian paradigm on the other (Harris, 1968, p. 881).

The first position Harris considers is that of **Leslie White** (1900-1975) who had studied with Thorstein Veblen, a member of the Chicago School (§ 4.1), the first to argue for the notion of technological determinism (Veblen, 1899) and followed several insights proposed by Alfred Kroeber, who created the notion of the "superorganic" (Kroeber, 1952). With *The Science of Culture* (1949), White, who was a convinced advocate of cultural determinism and clearly opposed the most orthodox positions of the culture and personality school (Peace, 2004), recognized the technological factors, and in particular humanity's ability to produce and manage different forms of power—the so-called "White's law", a fundamental law of cultural evolution (p. 333)—as mainly responsible for cultural processes (Moore, 2012, p. 161). Given a cultural system conceived as the sum of three overlying levels—a technological, a social, and a philosophical-symbolic level—White attributed a fundamental and primary causal role to the technological one, and a subordinate function to the second and third levels of the social and the philosophical-symbolic. Therefore, the technological factor «determines the form of social systems, and technology and society together determine the content and orientation of philosophy» (p. 334). According to White, technology is the key to understand the development and progress of culture. In this sense, he became the interpreter of a neo-evolutionist approach (White, 1959) that tried to overcome the ethno-centrism inherent in the first generation of anthropologists who belonged to the more orthodox evolutionist tradition (such as Lewis Morgan in the United States and Edward Taylor in England (Kaplan and Manners, 1972)), recognizing technology as the main cause of development of the social and philosophical factors in any cultural system.

The second speculative position integrated by Harris within cultural materialism is represented by **Julian Steward** (1902-1972), who had studied with Kroeber in Berkeley. Steward had amended the idea of cultural evolution by recognizing the importance of the environmental factors in the inherent process of change with which a certain culture evolves and develops (Kaplan and Manners, 1972, p. 75). The notion of cultural ecology—later defined by Harris as a subset of cultural materialism (Harris, 1968, p.

886)—conveys the relationship of mutual adaptation between culture and environment, thus «the interaction of physical, biological, and cultural features within a local or a unit of territory» (Steward, 1955, p. 30). On one side, Steward tries to recognize the environment's influence on cultural forms, on the other side he wants to understand how a certain culture ecologically adapts within a certain environment. Like Harris and White, in so doing he also recognized that material and technological factors play a relevant role in cultural development, particularly if considered in relation with the inherent processes of environmental adaptation and structural change. As the interpreter of an essentially holistic and systemic view of culture according to which every aspect is co-dependent with the others, where the environmental factors are considered in relation with the development of the cultural models, Steward did not refrain from assigning an active role to the forms of material culture precisely because they are the main interface of mediation between human biological sphere and environmental sphere (Kaplan and Manners, 1972, p. 77). Harris' materialist approach actually relies on the awareness that every cultural system results from a relationship of mutual interpenetration, and therefore of co-evolution, between human beings and the environment. The essence of cultural materialism, he writes «is that it directs attention to the interaction between behaviour and environment as mediated by the human organism and its cultural apparatus » (Harris, 1979, p. 888). Basically, humanity adapts to the wider environment precisely through culture. Humanity's ability to culturally adapt is precisely due to the acquisition of a complex material apparatus that considers both the natural and the historical-social environment.

Within this speculative frame, Edward Hall's approach is in line with the notion of cultural ecology proposed by Steward and integrated in Harris' materialism. He writes: «both man and his environment participate in molding each other» (Hall, 1966, p. 11). However, with this Hall explains that, according to a systemic logic, it is necessary to jointly consider all the expressive forms of human culture, thus all the "extensions of man" that can be related to the notion of material culture as well as the complex system of components that instead remain mostly hidden and relate to the sphere of attitudes, values, categories of thought, of the sensory world, including the arts (p. 99) and literature (p. 120), that he considers the keys to perception and represent the unconscious substrate of culture that impacts on creation of human experience and more in general of a vision of the world. Starting from the arguments in *Beyond Culture* (Hall, 1976), this cultural model—that describes an array of external elements visibly emerging in the features of a culture complemented by a wide array of equally influential elements deeply related to the former one but operating at a hidden, unconscious a level—would be basically borrowed by the intercultural studies as the "iceberg theory" (Brake et al., 1995; Katan, 1999). Hall's approach combines and mixes within a systemic view of culture both the material concept advocated by Harris and White and the cognitivist tradition founded by Boas. This is the essence of Hall's ecological approach—the intellectual relevance of which perhaps has not been fully recognized yet (Rogers, 2000)—according to which culture is conceived as a whole, a dynamic system, a coherent complex within which all the elements are deeply connected and therefore co-dependent. In conclusion, Hall should be credited for revealing, based on the ethnographic method and on an accurate meditation on the forms of communication, the continuous, circular, and retroactive relationship between humanity and our (material, cultural, and symbolic) extensions that a wide intellectual tradition, based on Edward Hall's approach, has defined as media ecology.

Edward Hall's main works
The Silent Language (1959)
The Hidden Dimension (1966)
Beyond Culture (1976)
The Dance of Life (1983)
An Anthropology of Everyday Life (1992)

Further readings
Birdwhistell R.L. (1952), *Introduction to Kinesics. An Annotation System for Analysis of Body Motion and Gesture*, University of Louisville Press, Louisville.
Bluedorn A.C. (1998), "An Interview with Anthropologist Edward T. Hall", *Journal of Management Inquiry*, 7, 2, pp. 109-115.
Harris M. (1968), The rise of anthropological theory. A history of theories of culture, Crowell, New York.

Harris M. (1968), *Cultural Materialism: the Struggle for a Science of Culture*, AltaMira Press, Walnut Creek, CA.

Rogers E.M. (2000), "The Extensions of Men. The Correspondence of Marshall McLuhan and Edward T. Hall", *Mass Communication and Society*, 3, 1, pp. 117-135.

Rogers E.M., Hart W.B., Miike Y. (2002), "Edward T. Hall and The History of Intercultural Communication", *Keio Communication Review*, 24, pp. 3-26.

Sapir E. (1921), *Language. An introduction to the study of speech*, Harcourt, New York.

Steward J.H. (1955), *The Theory of Culture Change. The methodology of multilinear evolution*, Univ. of Illinois Press, Urbana.

White L.A. (1949), *The science of culture. A study of man and civilization*, Farrar Straus, New York.

Whorf B.L. (1956), *Language, thought, and reality. Selected writings*, The MIT Press, Cambridge MA.

Winkin Y. e Leeds-Hurwitz W. (2013), *Erving Goffman. A Critical Introduction to Media and Communication Theory*, Peter Lang, New York.

Documentary films

Edward T. Hall (1989), Karl Kernberger.

5. European roots

5.1 The French scene

Although firmly rooted in North American cultural contexts, the intellectual tradition of media ecology effectively absorbed ideas and authors from a prolific European milieu. The multiplicity of substantial contributions from the European tradition is still the focus of many meditations on this field of study that have effectively tried to show how the European scene lent a powerful hand in confirming and expanding the relevance of the ecological approach to the study and understanding of media.

Within the French intellectual scene, one figure stands out for his enthusiastic embrace of media ecology and particularly for the similarities he expressed with the North American pioneers of the field. This figure is **Jacques Ellul** (1912-1994). An independent and in many ways solitary and discreet thinker, although no less committed to his craft, Ellul was skeptical towards a certain intellectual élite dominated by the Existentialists that, in turn, snubbed him. The remarkable attention he received from several American universities during the 1970s and 1980s certainly vindicated him.

The son of immigrants, Ellul mostly spent a modest childhood in Pessac, a small town in the French province not far from Bordeaux. During WWII and the years of economic crisis he fought for the Resistance movement all the while studying theology and law. For this reason, he had to wait until the war was over before he could obtain a teaching post in Roman law at the University of Bordeaux's Institute of Political Studies. With about fifty books translated into several languages, he was a quite prolific writer. As the author of the monumental volume, *History of*

Institutions (1955), written in a largely accessible language with a remarkable polemical approach, Ellul proposed a radical argument developed on a double level: that of theological studies—he was a Protestant Christian who operated within the Reformed Church—and that of the political-social studies he openly conducted from an anarchical and anti-capitalistic point of view (Troude-Chastenet, 1992). His ample and mostly provocative body of work, written with the goal of stimulating an individual awareness in his readers and his militancy in the National Liberation Movement during the troubled postwar years in France clearly reflect «an intellectual with a bold, practical, constantly dynamic approach» (Porquet, 2003, p. 14) who successfully expressed a critical, dialectical spirit free from ideological exaggerations; in other words, he was a free and realist outsider (Greenman et al., 2013, p. 12). These features render him an original and idiosyncratic thinker (Latouche, 1995, 2013), celebrated by the ecologist movement and even capable of drawing interest in the French no-global movement (Porquet, 2013, p. 221).

The main reason why media ecology has focused on Ellul—given he was included by William Kuhns in the group of the so-called post-industrial prophets, along with Mumford, Giedion, Innis, McLuhan, Wiener and Fuller (Kuhns, 1971)—is the concept of Technique, an element that constantly and transversally features in the French intellectual's entire opus, always with a capital T to indicate its relevant semantic meaning due to the political, economic, and social impact of technical progress that Ellul always considered with a cleverly critical spirit. Produced over about thirty years, the sequence of works devoted to the understanding of technological society ranges from *La technique ou l'enjeu du siècle* (1954) to *Le système technicien* (1977), until the last and in many ways terminal pamphlet, *Le Bluff technologique* (1988).

From Ellul's sociological-political point of view, Technique is a mostly independent entity that only leaves humans a leverage limited to a necessary process of awareness, a social conscience the French thinker would constantly insist on, and that saves him from the accusations of being a pessimist, fatalist, or Manichaean thinker often made by his critics (Kuhns, 1971, p. 82; Porquet, 2003, p. 18; Kluver, 2006, p. 107). It should be noted that Ellul never argued *against* Technique (1988, p. 9), and rather tried to *consider* Technique (Porquet, 2003, p. 47) by observing the mostly invisible phenomena that in the increasingly technologized modern world contribute to the substrate that potentially influences political, economic, and social processes. For Ellul, the scope of Technique is never limited to the merely material or instrumental apparatus of a society, or the perceivable expression of the various technologies. With its invisibility, as well as its pervasive presence, Technique rather embraces a network of conditioning that is deeply rooted in contemporary man and effectively influence any level of human life. For this reason, Technique penetrates even the most remote recesses of individual and collective life. Ellul would describe this situation as the hidden face of the technical society (1954). For this reason, more than Technique itself, his real concern is the reaction of human conscience to its unstoppable development (Kuvler, 2006, p. 108). Ellul's endeavour can be seen as an attempt to overcome the habitual and easy refrain of technological determinism (Flichy, 1995, p. 37). The author's primary goal is to promote critical awareness of human progress beyond the unconscious mechanisms of conditioning; a perspective sometimes impertinent and defiant precisely because it results from an act of awareness in considering technology.

In the trilogy's second book, *Le système technicien* (1977), the vision introduced in the previous volume becomes increasingly detailed. Ellul argues that the technological world has transcended its role as a primary factor for society (p. 75) to become an actual system—the "technological system" (p. 101): «Technology is not content with *being*, or in our world, with being the *principal or determining factor.* Technology has become a system» (p. 15). Therefore, each element of this system ‚«an organized whole» (p. 32), is in close connection with the other, in a relation of mutual influence based on an open, dynamic, and multivalent logic. And, as a system that is widespread, innervated, and rooted in society, it has ceased to be a merely external, human-made, instrumental apparatus, as such more or less controllable, and has become a new environment of life for humanity that can embrace, shape, and direct our needs, choices, and our very interpretive horizons. Therefore, Ellul articulated a new concept of technology, viewed as an environment and a system (Séris, 1994, p. 51; Latouche, 1995, p. 62). It «is far more of a mediation than an instrument» (p. 55), he explains. «Not only a means, but a universe of means; in the original sense of *Universum*: both inclusive and total» (Ellul, 1977, p. 57). And further, «having become a *universum* of means and media, technology is in fact the environment of man. The mediations are so generalized, extended, multiplied, that they have come to make up a new universe; we have witnessed the emergence of the "technological environment"» (pp. 60-61). Closing this argument, he writes: «Now, as modern men, we are called upon not to employ technologies, but to hue with and among them in their environment» (p. 66). Ellul's arguments are closely in agreement with the insights proposed a few years earlier in North America by an interpreter of Technique, Lewis Mumford (p. 34; § 2.1), with his concept of "mega-machine" (Mumford, 1967, p. 317; Latouche, 1995), or by an observer of media forms like McLuhan (Ellul, 1977, p. 34; § 3.2) whose concept of "global village" (McLuhan and Fiore, 1968) mirrors, in many ways, the systemic approach proposed by Ellul (McLuhan M. and McLuhan E., 1988).

One last consideration on Ellul's research touches on a work that enjoyed wide circulation among North American scholars, *Propagandes* (Ellul, 1962), within which the author approaches the specific area of communication media, considered as a subgroup of the technical system, and views the function of information media as a privileged environment where the slippery processes and mechanisms of propaganda effectively produce social and political results (Strate, 2006, p. 74; Greenman et al., 2013, p. 38); a modern Babel of communication (Sfez, 1990, p. 164). The author later returned to this subject (Ellul, 1987, 1988) in connection with the propagation of new information technology that he though was capable of gaining increasingly flowing, absorbing, and all-engaging forms that would effectively overcome the old clichés of mechanization and industrialism and become a new and disruptive immaterial power in the global flow of information that, as such, would be ready once more to transform the cultural environment of contemporary society. At this point, the close connection between Ellul and the North American intellectual tradition that underlies the study of media ecology becomes entirely clear, as further evidenced by connections with the work of Innis (Gozzi, 2000), Ong (Kuvler, 2006), and Postman (Strate 2006), as well as with the more general approach of media theory (Christians and Real, 1979).

On another side of twentieth century humanistic thought, the anthropological perspective, the rich tradition of French studies provided media ecology with an array of valuable interpretative vantage points for the understanding of human culture and the mediating relation that has always existed between human beings and our environment. An essential contribution in this sense was provided by the French ethnologist and paleontologist **André Leroi-Gourhan** (1911-1986). A cultivated and polyglot intellectual who had studied with Marcel Mauss in line with Levi-Strauss' structuralist approach, he was a professor at the Sorbonne and the Collège de France and, although he never abandoned his activity as a researcher, was as well an expert of prehistoric art and archeology of cultures of the Pacific Ocean.

Being particularly interested in material culture, Leroi-Gourhan focused his concerns on the relationship between technology and culture, based on which he initiated an actual intellectual school within French anthropology called School of Cultural Technology (Flichy, 1995, p. 80; Warnier, 1999, p. 70). His fundamental approach was aimed at viewing the material world of human cultures as a system; a technical system closely related to the communication and socialization skills inherent in the human species. Based on the insights provided by Marcel Mauss, the issues of the human body, gestures, and language become the key elements of the technical system, a notion that Leroi-Gourhan pioneered along with others. In his view, the system of material artefacts should be seen as a kind of manifestation of the human interior dimension in the natural environment's exterior dimension. Therefore, the "morphology of technology" that underlies the relationship between *Man and Matter* (1943) exists in the reflection of «a double movement, interior and exterior» (p. 13). In other words, the technical apparatus that provides humans with the power to shape their own environment takes the form of a prosthesis, an extension. And these skills, or the biological and symbolic dimension inherent in the human species, put humans in the position to surround himself with a system of prostheses so powerful that it is just as important as the environmental factor in defining the biological as well as cultural and social development.

As Leroi-Gourhan argued in a later study, *Gesture and Speech* (1964), over the long history of human evolution, the features of gestuality, or any physical and body function, just like the very act of phonation, has the ability to communicate with others according to a process that he describes as «the organic oozing into the extraorganic» (p. 270). Once "the gesture" has oozed out or become exterior, it moves into the prosthetic sphere; therefore, tools free the hand and shape a new environment of development, a new human habitat ruled by the domination of the material world over the organic world. Equally, through language, and then writing, "the word" oozes into the essentially biological domain, expands and frees itself due to «our unique ability to transfer our memory to a social organism outside ourselves» (p. 277).

Leroi-Gourhan's systemic approach and methodological rigour in addressing the relationship between technology and culture achieves results that are in many ways similar to those reached by Edward Hall (§ 4.3) in the sphere of cultural anthropology in the US. The idea of technology as an extension of humans, broadly picked up by McLuhan himself (§ 3.2), provides an interpretative frame that is useful to understanding the complexity of humanity's relationship with the world and finds an array of brilliant solutions in the ecological approach viewed or, more specifically, an ecology of technology.

An additional consideration on the French intellectual tradition and its points of contact with media ecology should be made about *Les Annales*, an intellectual school that renewed the historiographic tradition during the twentieth century, and in particular about **Fernand Braudel** (1902-1985), one of its most eminent members. In his monumental *Capitalism and Material Life* (1967) Braudel addresses the relationship between technology and culture by placing it in the background of the great cycles of the modern age. As he peremptorily argues: «Everything is technology» (p. 253). Human beings have always mediated their relationship with the world through technical-instrumental interventions—of a both material and an ideational type—and, in so doing, has effectively created the conditions for the development of the renewal process that is human culture. In other words, Braudel argues that culture is incorporated into technology, or in the «patient and monotonous efforts to make a mark upon the external world» (p. 250), that mirror a slow and constant «labor of man over man» (p. 250), according to a logic of circularity and mutual causality (and not of mere subordination of one part or the other, as argued by the deterministic approaches) that can be variously compared to the environmental and systemic approach adopted by media ecology.

One last, brief consideration should be finally made about two scholars who worked in French academic contexts and in many ways supported the North American tradition of media ecology. The first one is the Swiss-born **René Berger** (1915-2009), who authored many essays including *Art et Communication* (1972) and *Le nouveau Golem* (1991), that aimed to isolate symbolic aspects in expressive forms of art that could determine meaningful changes in cultural environments. An approach that can be considered as similar in many ways is that adopted by another cosmopolitan intellectual, **Vilém Flusser** (1920-1991), who worked for a long time in French academia. He was a Czech-born philosopher and a brilliant interpreter of a phenomenology of visual languages. His book, *The Culture of the Media* (1992), was developed from an array of analyses of the artistic processes. Previous to this work, *Towards a Philosophy of Photography* (1983) and *Images* (1985) focused on the impacts or humanity's way of relating to the new social environment created by the media and the perceptual mechanisms of contemporary humanity.

Jacque Ellul's and André Leroi-Gourhan's main works
    The Technological Society (1954), Jacques Ellul
    Propaganda (1962), Jacques Ellul
    The Technological System (1977), Jacques Ellul
    The Technological Bluff (1988), Jacques Ellul
    Man and Matter (1943), André Leroi-Gourhan
    Gesture and Speech (1964), André Leroi-Gourhan

Further readings
Christians C.G. e Real M.R. (1979), "Jacques Ellul's Contributions to Critical Media Theory", *Journal of Communication*, 29, 1, pp. 83-93.
Gozzi R. (2000), "Jacques Ellul on Technique, Media, and the Spirit", *New Jersey Journal of Communication*, 8, 1, pp. 79-90.
Jerónimo H.M., Garcia J.L., Mitcham C. (2013), *Jacques Ellul and the Technological Society in the 21st Century*, Springer, New York.
Greenman J.P., Schuchardt R.M., Toly N.J. (2013), *Understanding Jacques Ellul*, James Clarke & co. Cambridge, UK.
Kluver R. (2006), "Jacques Ellul: Technique, Propaganda, and Modern Media", in Lum C.M.K., ed., *Perspectives on Culture, Technology and Communication: The Media Ecology Tradition*, Hampton Press, Cresskill, NJ, pp. 97-116.
Show J.M. (2014), *Illusions of Freedom: Thomas Merton and Jacques Ellul on Technology and the Human Condition*, Wipf and Stock, Eugene, OR.

5.2 The German tradition

The study of the similarities and convergence between the tradition of North American scholarship and European academia in the realm of media ecology must inevitably consider Germany, which is, in many ways, the cradle of humanistic and philosophical thought. Intellectual engagement with a particular author is required, if nothing else because he was one of the most brilliant and original thinkers of the twentieth century who provided a host of extraordinary cultural analyses about his time including countless insightful meditations on the media and on the expressive forms of human culture viewed from a systemic perspective. This author was **Walter Benjamin** (1892-1940), who can hardly be classified if not by relying on a long list of definitions, all of them partial given the scope of his intellectual legacy. He was a historian, a philosopher, a literary critic, as well as a writer, a broadcaster for the radio, a translator, a reviewer, an expert of Jewish mysticism and Messianism, an observer of urban landscapes, deeply curious of the most original cultural phenomena of his time from experimental theatre to figurative art, from cinema to photography, with a range of other interests including Baroque art, critical theory, and Marxist ideology. This multitude of themes, concepts and interests, his ability to think in terms of *constellations*—an allegorical image that fully conveys the sense of Benjamin's approach—and his ability to find original connections between heterogeneous forms of knowledge reveal a key methodological meaning that project Benjamin as an extremely attractive figure for the intellectual tradition of media ecology (Strate, 2006, p. 48) who developed the interweaving of disciplines and forms of knowledge as a distinctive features of his approach (Lum, 2006).

Born in Charlottenburg, a wealthy district of Berlin, Benjamin had German-Jewish origins. Coming from a rich family, he had a comfortable childhood only marred by a poor health and by the monotonous bourgeois life of the time. Driven by a clear interest for educational issues, the young Benjamin enlisted in a youth reformist movement called *Jugendbewegung* within which he was also active as a graduate student at the Freiburg University where in the meantime he had enrolled in the Philosophy department. The outbreak of the First World War, emerging nationalist claims, and the sacrifice of thousands of young soldiers who had enlisted in the army to defend their homeland stifled the idealist drive of the young Benjamin who, as a result, diverted his focus on the study of the Jewish philosophical tradition. Having returned to Berlin, he had the opportunity to follow Georg Simmel's lectures. Subsequently, he continued his studies in Munich and Frankfurt. The years following the war coincided with a massive disappointment for the promising young scholar who failed to qualify for a habilitation teaching credential and as a result saw his ambitions for an academic career vanish. From that moment on, Benjamin «would remain an intellectual outsider for the rest of his life» (Gilloch, 2002, p. 28).

That was the beginning of a long period of collaborations within the Berlin literary milieu for the young Benjamin who, as a result, would lead a life of financial uncertainty and lack of stability due to his occasional and underpaid jobs. During that period, he met Theodor Adorno with whom he established a lasting friendship in spite of their frequent differences about Marxist doctrine. It was also the time when Benjamin, either as a translator or as a reviewer, came to read the works of the greatest European writers, from Proust to Kafka, from Baudelaire to Brecht. With Brecht in particular, he felt a close intellectual kinship. Therefore, it was a time of fruitful insights and intense activity as a writer that would lead him to develop an original and innovative approach to writing—sometimes enigmatic, as well as uneven, inconsistent, disjointed—full of aphorisms, quotations, and fragments that convey an unparalleled intellectual voraciousness and critical acumen.

Between the 1920s and 1930s, Benjamin nurtured a particular interest for modern capitalism and Marxist criticism through a host of meditations about the fate of art, cultural forms, and social spaces. He became close to Max Horkheimer and authored several philosophical works including the celebrated *The Work of Art in the Age of Mechanical Reproduction* (1935) that became a classic text of media theory. This experience as a writer would lead him to develop a passion for the study and, in particular, for the reasoned observation of urban and metropolitan environments. For this reason, during that time he travelled extensively, and visited Moscow, Naples, and particularly Paris, where he developed his celebrated study about the *passages*, the French capital's commercial arcades that symbolize capitalist consumerism as a «panoramic, kaleidoscopic exploration of the fashions and phantasmagoria of the city» (Gilloch, 2002, p. 30). It was in Paris, in 1933, that he temporarily found shelter after fleeing Nazi persecution, until 1940, when the city was invaded by the Germans and he had to flee further south at the Spanish border in an attempt to reach Adorno and Horkheimer in the United States. When he failed to pass the border in Port Bou, he committed suicide under unclear circumstances. He was only 48 years old.

Benjamin's extensive work, constituted of a constellation of articles, notes, essays, reviews and travel reports, reveals and anticipates several insights that now belong to the theoretical and methodological foundations of media ecology. Such a heritage is the result of Benjamin's attempt to explore a host of cultural phenomena and experiences of the modern condition with no pretense to formulate any final judgments, but rather by combining ideas and meditations in a systemic approach that was open and provisional, although clear and strict in methodological terms. This is a first element of affinity between Benjamin—«an aesthetic, polytechnic and experimental engineer» (Gilloch, 2002, p. 10)—and media ecology that nonetheless is much more than a mere convergence in terms of method. The systemic logic is indeed what seems to have inspired the German thinker to formulate a host of enlightening meditations about the meaning of technology in the modern age that emerge from the pages of the *The Work of Art*'s first draft; thus, the version preceding the canonical publication.

Benjamin finds two separate ways of conceptualizing the relationship between human beings and technology. During the archaic ages, what Benjamin defines as «first technology» (Benjamin, 1935, p. 25), there is a mainly instrumental meaning of technology as an almost magical tool developed in an attempt to dominate nature, whereas in the modern age the «second technology» acquires an environmental kind of value. Due to its machinic outlook, in many ways autonomous and independent, this technique frees humans from the intention to dominate nature, aiming instead to establish «an interplay between nature and humanity» (*id.*). Therefore, what Benjamin sees is a substantial balance between natural and manmade spheres, increasingly closer to each other, according to an approach that views technology as an element that connects human beings and nature, «a system in which the mastering of elementary social forces is a precondition for playing with natural forces» (*id.*), thus a new environment created by humans—a second nature—within which they live and constantly put themselves in play. In other words, although this avowedly means simplifying a complex and articulated approach, Benjamin offers a systemic view of modern technology that highlights its positive potential—oft criticized by the members of the Frankfurt School—and implies that technology may have a revolutionary role in freeing the individual and stimulating a deeper critical conscience about the new playground where the relationship between human and nature takes place. As he argued: «The more the collective makes the second technology its own, the more tangible it becomes for the individuals belonging to the collective» (*id.*). Therefore, modern individuals live in a new technical environment. Benjamin thought this environment had a key social function, quite similar to the one defined by the school of historical materialism that he felt quite close to all while trying to neutralize its dialectical narrow-mindedness.

On the subject of the media, Benjamin's meditations—developed across a host of texts mostly written during the 1930s (Jennings et al., 2008)—emerge as particularly useful in defining some foundations of the framework of modern media ecology as articulated by the North American pioneers. First of all, Benjamin was perhaps the first scholar to overcome a view that only considered media as communication languages, and embraced instead the expressive forms of human culture in their entirety (p. 3) by including the means of representation belonging to the arts—painting, photography, cinema—and by extending them to the expressions of cultural industry—theatre, live performance, music, and radio (a new medium at the time)—without forgetting all the "high" and "low" forms of human culture: literature, architecture, technological devices, mass phenomena, to even include colour, «a pure property of no substance» (Benjamin, 1915, p. 92) and recreational drugs that could influence the individual and collective processes of perception and sense. This is an early hint of the originality of Benjamin's media theory that embraces all the cultural processes triggering a transformation of human cognitive and sensory apparatus in a kind of psycho-perceptive rearrangement of the individual. The arguments presented by Benjamin come from the fields of photography—*A short history of photography* (Benjamin, 1931, p. 225)—and cinema—*Discussion on Russian cinema* (1927, p. 256) in particular.

Already recognized as a «star in the current academic firmament» (Gilloch, 2002, p. 22), Benjamin should also be credited as a pioneer of media aesthetics. Following on the steps of some of the fathers of formal aesthetics, the representatives of the so-called Vienna School, such as Riegl and Wölfflin (Tatarkiewicz, 1975), he introduced an innovative idea of a medium as inherently capable of influencing the forms of perception and experience. Such transforming action of the medium also reveals the historically determined nature of human perceptive and sensory models. As he argued: «Just as the entire mode of existence of human collectives changes over long historical periods, so too does their mode of perception» (Benjamin, 1935, p. 24). And: «The way in which human perception is organized – the *medium* in which it occurs – is conditioned not only by nature but by history» (*id.*). This points once and for all at a clear coincidence within Benjamin's approach between media theory and perception theory, in a way that in many ways anticipates McLuhan's insights about human sensorium (§ 3.2)—not coincidentally, McLuhan, like Benjamin, was interested in the thinkers of the Vienna School—and Walter Ong's insights about the so-called historicization of sensorium (§ 3.3) and, finally, Edward Hall's insights about cultural and sensory relativism (§ 4.3).

A further consideration about the relevance of Benjamin's theories for the pioneers of media ecology concerns an intellectual current that can be related to both Edward Hall and Neil Postman (§ 2.3). This is the body of theories that can be traced to linguistic relativism. The media dimension of language is indeed a focus of Benjamin's intellectual trajectory developed between literary criticism and the theological suggestions of the Jewish tradition that contains a reference to Wilhelm von Humboldt (1820), one of the pioneers of linguistic relativism. Benjamin's approach to language is not necessarily confined to the transmission of messages or content and, instead focuses on the idea of language as a medium that communicates itself by expressing a certain thing in specifically linguistic terms. With this, Benjamin seems to have paved the way also to a speculative approach that views media as languages with their own universe of sense that can influence the contents they convey. This view can be recognized in both British New Criticism (§ 5.3) and, in a more provocative form, in McLuhan's catchphrase "the medium is the message" (McLuhan, 1964a, p. 29).

A further derivation from the ideas of Benjamin, once again rooted in the ground of the cultural forms he explored in some pages of *The Work of Art* (Benjamin, 1935, p. 26), emerges with reference to McLuhan's as well as to Edward Hall's thought. This is the concept of "innervation", often analyzed by Benjamin's scholars, that in many ways anticipated the idea of media as extensions, or prostheses, or continuations (Flayhan, 2002), introduced by Hall (1959, p. 26), and later brought to the forefront by McLuhan (1962, p. 26), while also present during the same years in the intellectual toolkit of others including Leroi-Gourhan (§ 5.1). Benjamin argues that, as media stimulate the human sensory sphere—an action fully performed by the "second technology" (Benjamin, 1935, p. 25)—they become actual organs of the collective that extend the individual organs in a relationship of mutual integration as well as of continuity between the psycho-perceptive sphere of human beings and the extended, protracted, innervated sphere of the environment. This consideration underlies Benjamin's meditations collected in the famous *Passages* and in his works about architecture and the urban landscape (including *Paris, Capital of the Nineteenth Century* (Benjamin, 1935, p. 372)) that view the city as a medium of modern thinking, the extension of the collective unconscious, an environment that can trigger new ways of establishing human experience. There are, in this, peculiar similarities with the ecological tradition of Chicago (§ 4.1) and with the insights proposed by Lewis Mumford in the intellectual context of New York (§ 2.1). Once more, Benjamin emerges as an undisputed pioneer of the systemic view of the symbolic and material human universe—an environment, a media constellation—that eventually found a more effective, although far from fully recognized, achievement in the intellectual tradition of media ecology.

The German philosophical tradition offers at least a few other key figures that can be recognized for their crucial conceptual contributions to the North American field of media ecology. The first one is **Ernst Cassirer** (1874-1945), an undisputed pioneer of the philosophy of culture (Skidelsky, 2008) whose intellectual heritage represents the argumentative backdrop of the meditations developed in the US by Susan Langer about the expressive forms of human culture (§ 2.2), and in particular on the symbolic forms (Cassirer, 1923-29) that represent the core of the Cassirer's inquiry. Born into a Jewish family, Cassirer was forced to leave Germany to escape Nazi persecution and take refuge first in Sweden and later in the United States. In step with the so-called Marburg School and the philosophical tradition of Neo-Kantism, Cassirer thought the symbolic aspects of human culture provide an access to understand its many expressive forms, including language, myth, religion, art, and by extension, media in their widest meaning. In Cassirer's view, our human cultural environment is the conceptual foundation that gives meaning to our experience interacting with and interpreting the world. The key to this is precisely the symbolic dimension, the ability to create symbols that is inherent in human beings—humanity as *animal symbolicum* according to the famous definition (Cassirer, 1944, p. 49)—and that is revealed through the expressive, material or ideational forms of human culture, which, precisely for their symbolic potential, induce a constant reconfiguration of experience. Such a symbolic dimension acquires a systemic value for Cassirer, as a "symbolic system" (p. 47) that can completely transform human life. Cassirer writes: «As compared with the other animals man lives not merely in a broader reality; he lives, so to speak, in a new dimension of reality. [...] no longer in a merely physical universe, man lives in a symbolic universe» (*id.*). This dimension of reality offers man a constantly new environment that influences and shapes human culture. In addition, Cassirer relies on the original combination *forma formans/forma formata* (1930) to explain the interaction between humanity and our symbolic environment. These processes occur within a sort of artificial mediation, a mutual formative process of an aesthetical nature that leads human beings to *shape* their cultural forms, their symbols, and at the same to be *shaped* by them. In other words, the media, as symbolic forms of human culture, are "shaping energies" (2010, p. 36), or energies that can shape humanity, but at the same time are shaped by humanity, based on a circular, systemic, environmental process. These arguments explain the close relationship between Cassirer's thought, conceived as an ecology of culture, an ecology of symbolic forms, and the intellectual tradition of media ecology.

A second key figure who can help understanding the special systemic relationship underlying the connection between humanity and our cultural forms is **Ernst Kapp** (1808-1896), a geographer, philosopher, and an unappreciated thinker who belonged to the German Romantic movement. A pioneer of the philosophy of technology, Kapp was perhaps one of the very first thinkers to conceptualize the cognitive and sensory sphere (Curtis, 1978, p. 61; Brey, 2000, p. 59) as a process that is so powerful it can shape a new living environment for the individual and the collectivity and deeply impact on the forms of human experience and social reality (Kapp, 1877).

A quick mention to the sociological sphere of the German humanistic tradition leads instead to the influence exerted by **Georg Simmel** (1858-1918), and his considerations about the metropolitan experience with reference to thinkers who belonged to the so-called Ecological School of Chicago (§ 4.1), in particular

Albion Small, William Thomas and Robert Park, and more in general to the North-American tradition of media studies (Anton, 2013). In his classic, *The Metropolis and Mental Life* (1903), he views the urban environment as a medium from which the forms of social life and human experience develop and in the frame of which the analysis of metropolitan modernity becomes useful to understanding media.

The clear connections between German sociology and media ecology are also reflected in the work of **Niklas Luhmann** (1927-1998). Several works—*Social systems* (1984), *Ecological Communication* (1986), *The Reality of the Mass Media* (1996)—show his belief in a systemic view of the social environment that he thought is established by the communication processes, an actual substrate of the development of human culture that can shape a complex environment within which the social reality in turn is shaped. In his work, Luhmann also borrowed some considerations made by Eric Havelock and Walter Ong (§ 3.3) about the role of the press in the process of establishment of social systems.

One last figure from the German intellectual milieu is **Friedrich Kittler** (1943-2011), who was in many ways a transversal thinker who attracted the interest of several North American scholars. In the great number of essays he authored about cultural and communication forms—the best known of which is *Gramophone, Film, Typewriter* (Kittler, 1986)—Kittler incorporated insights and approaches from the tradition of media ecology and combined them with Foucault's post-structuralist analysis (such as the concept of "social system" that features in Foucault's approach (Foucault, 1975)) to recognize the keys to understand contemporary society in the influence media have on perception and learning. In his review of the history of technological practices and their impact on cultural production as divided into three major time cycles (Kittler, 1990), the German scholar recognized the mediation they performed in the interaction between the individuals and in shaping new perceptive maps (Winthrop-Young, 2011). The fact that Kittler views the concept of medium as closely related to the theory of sensory perception (Kittler, 2009, p. 24) clearly places him on the fruitful axis of media aesthetics and philosophy that also nurtured the media ecological approach. Finally, he was also particularly interested in the city, and here Lewis Mumford's influence looms large (§ 2.1), almost in an attempt to achieve a marriage between the North American and the European intellectual traditions on the fertile ground of media ecology.

Main works
    The Metropolis and Mental Life (1903), Georg Simmel
    The Philosophy of Symbolic Forms (1923-29), Ernst Cassirer
    The Work of Art in the Age of Mechanical Reproduction (1935), Walter Benjamin
    Illuminations: Essays and Reflections (1961), Walter Benjamin
    Social systems (1984), Niklas Luhmann
    Ecological Communication (1986), Niklas Luhmann
    The Reality of the Mass Media (1996), Niklas Luhmann
    Discourse Networks 1800/1900 (1985), Friedrich Kittler
    Gramophone Film Typewriter (1986), Friedrich Kittler

Further readings
Eiland H., Jennings M.W. (2014), *Walter Benjamin: A Critical Life*, Harvard University Press, Cambridge UK.
Friesen N., Cavell R. (2016), *Media Transatlantic: Developments in Media and Communication Studies between North American and German-speaking Europe*, Springer, London.
Gilloch G. (2002), *Walter Benjamin: Critical Constellations*, Polity Press, Cambridge UK.
Jennings M.W., Doherty B., Lebin T.Y., eds. (2008), *The Work of Art in the Age of Technological Reproduction and Other Writings on Media*, Harvard University Press, Cambridge MA.
Leslie E. (2008), *Walter Benjamin*, Reaktion Books, London.
Skidelsky E. (2008), *Ernst Cassirer. The Last Philosopher of Culture*, Princeton University Press, Princeton, NJ.
Winthrop-Young G., Gane N. (2006), Special Issue: Friedrich Kittler, *Theory, Culture & Society*, 23, 7-8.
Winthrop-Young G. (2011), *Kittler and the Media*, Polity Press, Cambridge UK.

5.3 The British context

The influence of the British intellectual milieu on the media ecology tradition is particularly recognizable in three major spheres of twentieth century humanistic thought: literature, anthropology, and sociology.

In the case of literature, the seat of this influence was Cambridge which witnessed during the 1920s and 1930s a major turning point for literary criticism that at the time relied on the Victorian canon and the stylistic tenets of the most conformist academic tradition. This turning point was mainly promoted by the members of what came to be known as the Cambridge School, a group of intellectuals who would play an important role within the European side of the critical-literary trend called New Criticism, developed at the time between England and the United States.

The moving force of the Cambridge School was **Ivor A. Richards** (1893-1969). A philosopher and a linguist, an expert of literary criticism and psychology, Richards tried to combine a scientific approach with a method of critical analysis that embraced aesthetics, rhetoric, and semiotics (Chatterjee, 2002). The results of his efforts were presented in his best-known work, *The Principles of Literary Criticism* (Richards, 1924).

Another key figure of this school was **Charles K. Ogden** (1889-1957), who co-authored *The Meaning of Meaning* with Richards (Richards and Ogden, 1923), a fundamental work for the philosophy of language and a survey of the role of language in human thought and in human life in general. Clearly indebted to Charles S. Peirce's semiotic approach, Richards and Ogden's work surveys the relationship between mental processes, symbols, and reality, and underlines the symbolic dimension's key role in defining the meaning of any communication act. Due to its symbolic dimension, language incorporates an array of cultural issues that influence the way of interpreting reality. Recognizable in any human expressive form, not just poetry and literature, such role of language performs a peculiar action in that it extends the meaning of things. In other words, all media are carriers of meaning, beyond the contents they convey.

Frank R. Leavis (1895-1978) was another member of the Cambridge School who gave an important contribution aimed at renewing the idea of cultural tradition and applying the methods of literary criticism, at the time almost exclusively used to interpret élite expressive forms, to mass culture expressive forms as well. In *Culture and Environment* (Leavis and Thompson, 1933), Leavis argues that language is more than a medium used by society to share its culture and, instead, proposes to consider its mediating function between the individual and his social context. In other words, language can influence the very processes of interpretation and attribution of meaning. Therefore, language is a medium, and as such it performs an environmental action over the contexts it mediates. On the other side, every medium is a language, and as such it commands certain symbolic features that can determine the meaning given to a certain reality in a certain environment. All of these considerations testify to the remarkable contribution provided by the Cambridge School to media ecology. Indeed, the interpretive approach proposed by Richards, Ogden and Leavis would influence the survey developed by Postman (§ 2.3) and McLuhan (§ 3.2) about the linguistic nature of media, as well as Ong's study of the role of language in the development of human thought (§ 3.3) and Langer's work on the symbolic function of the linguistic acts (§ 2.2).

A particularly interesting contribution in the field of anthropology was provided by **Jack Goody** (1919-2015). Goody, who had studied English Literature at Cambridge, became a prolific and versatile author (with as many as thirty books translated into various languages) with interests in a wide array of fields including social anthropology and ethnography, the history of philosophical thought, and political doctrine. Starting with his first and most important work, *The Consequences of Literacy*, co-authored with Ian Watt (Goody and Watt, 1963), Goody pursued a wide-ranging cross-disciplinary survey aimed at studying the effects of writing on social organization and on the human cognitive processes. Following on the steps of the research developed by Eric Havelock (§ 3.3) about the deep changes that occurred in ancient Greece with the passage from oral to written culture, and supported by an ethnographic activity conducted in India, China, and Western

Africa (Guichard, 2012), Goody formulated a general kind of axiom that projected literacy as a key element in the processes of civilization of humankind. He also recognized a special role to writing within human evolution due to its specific power to promote an expansion of critical activity and logical thinking. In his words, writing «increased the potentiality for cumulative knowledge, especially knowledge of an abstract kind, because it changed the nature of communication beyond that of face-to-face contact as well as the system for the storage of information» (Goody, 1977, p. 48). Therefore, Goody extensively argued that across the history of human culture, just like in the illiterate populations he studied during his field research, the advent of writing—as an actual «technology of the intellect» (1987, p. 265)—had a deep impact on the way of preserving tradition, storing knowledge and transmitting memory, all while recognizing orality as a major form of human interaction (Olson and Cole, 2006). In addition, beyond the specific realm of the alphabetic medium, the transformation of the communication processes considered in their entirety is a defining element in the transformation of the entire society in any historical or cultural age. Goody explains that: «Culture, after all, is a series of communicative acts, and differences in the mode of communication are often as important as differences in the mode of production, for they involve developments in the storing, analysis, and creation of human knowledge, as well as the relationships between the individuals involved» (Goody, 1977, p. 48). To put it another way, Goody argues that communication systems, the sharing of values and symbols and the transmission of memory, are as vital in the development of a society as the means of production or material technologies. In this way, Goody's work plays a central role in supporting the important study of orality and literacy, a crucial theoretical core of media ecology (Lum, 2006, p. 35; Strate, 2006, p. 41). Therefore, not only can his research be recognized as similar to that developed by Havelock about the ancient Greek world, it also seems to be on the same wavelength as Harold Innis' studies on the monopolies of knowledge (§ 3.1) and as those of McLuhan, Ong, Eisenstein on the specific issue of the cultural role played by print during the Renaissance and its impact on the social life of modern humanity (§ 3.3).

Speaking of sociological research based out of the UK and its influence on the North American pioneers of media ecology, one final reference should be made to the Scottish biologist **Patrick Geddes** (1854-1932). An encyclopedic thinker who successfully combined heterogeneous interests, from biology to botany, from pedagogy to architecture, Geddes is considered a pioneer of urban sociology due to his role in founding the Outlook Tower in Edinburgh in 1892. A peculiar and original observatory on the city, a research outpost on social sciences, the Outlook Tower was considered at the time as the world's very first sociological laboratory (Mattelart, 1994, p. 161). His futuristic and at time eclectic insights reflect an approach that sought to promote the propagation of knowledge based on a syncretic and holistic perspective revolving around the concept of human ecology defined by Geddes himself (Geddes, 1915; Meller, 1990), although previously introduced by the American biologist Ellen Richards (1907) and later picked up by some members of the Chicago School (McKenzie, 1925; Park, 1936; Wirth, 1945; § 4.1). Geddes' genius and visionary personality, his ecological approach to the phenomena of human culture would greatly influence Lewis Mumford (§ 2.1), who often expressed his gratitude towards the unconventional Scottish scholar (Miller, 1989), also testified by a close correspondence (Novak, 1995). The ecological perspective that Mumford borrowed from his brilliant mentor was ultimately the result of an intellectual heritage that is still very much alive and fruitful in that heterogeneous and vibrant field of study, media ecology.

Main works
    Cities in evolution (1915), Patrick Geddes
    The Principles of Literary Criticism (1924), Ivor Richards
    The Meaning of Meaning (1923), Ivor Richards and Charles Ogden
    Culture and Environment (1933), Frank Leavis and Denys Thompson
    The Consequences of Literacy (1963), Jack Goody and Ian Watt
    The Domestication of the Savage Mind (1977), Jack Goody
    The Interface Between the Written and the Oral (1987), Jack Goody

Further readings
Boardman P. (1944), *Patrick Geddes, maker of the future*, University of North Carolina Press, Chapel Hill.
Meller H.E. (1990), *Patrick Geddes. Social Evolutionist and City Planner*, Routledge, London.
Olson D.R., Cole M., eds. (2006), *Technology, literacy, and the evolution of society. Implications of the work of Jack Goody*, Lawrence Erlbaum, London.
Stephen W. (2004), *Think global, act local: The life and legacy of Patrick Geddes*, Luath Press, Edinburgh.
Welter V., Lawson, J., eds. (2000), *The city after Patrick Geddes*, Peter Lang, Oxford.
Welter V. (2002), *Biopolis. Patrick Geddes and the city of life*, MIT Press, Cambridge, MA.

6. Media Ecology today

A truly staggering amount of studies have been published in North America since the formal establishment of media ecology as a field of study promoted by Neil Postman in 1968. A wide body of works developed with the aim of systematizing a constantly changing phenomenon should be added to the historiographical sources previously listed. These works were mainly published in the United States and in Canada, the two major hubs of this intellectual endeavour.

Starting with the United States, a large group of scholars have worked on and developed Neil Postman's intellectual heritage. As mentioned above, a particularly relevant role has been played by Lance Strate, who authored several systematic studies about media ecology as well as a contemporary review of Neil Postman's work (Strate, 2014). Gary Gumpert, a longtime collaborator of Postman, also authored an important essay about the relationship between media and cultural industry viewed through an ecological perspective (Gumpert, 1988). Paul Levinson, who studied under Postman, provided an interpretive key to understand the evolution of contemporary media (Levinson, 1997), as well as a brilliant and insightful assessment of McLuhan's thought (1999). Thom Gencarelli illustrated Postman's role in media ecology (2000, 2006). Joshua Meyrowitz, who studied with Postman and Gumpert, is, instead, perhaps the best-known member of the group due to his work *No Sense of Place* (1985), unanimously considered as a classic of media studies that frames a wide array of elements such as Innis' historical vision, McLuhan's ecological approach, Goffman's interactionism, as well as a host of other brilliant insights.

Other scholars who worked outside the New York scene can be related to the tradition of media ecology. These include David

Altheide, who authored a remarkable essay about the ecology of communication (1995) influenced by the interactionist perspective, Carolyn Marvin (1988), who approached the history of media from an evolutionist perspective, and Daniel Czitrom (1982), who developed a well-documented study about the work of Dewey, Cooley, Park, Innis, and McLuhan. Other scholars have worked specifically on McLuhan. These include Paul Grosswiler (1998), Jeffrey Schnapp (2012) and two academics, Richard Grusin and David Bolter (1999), who are well-known for introducing the concept of "remediation". Bolter also worked on the relationship between orality and writing inaugurated by Walter Ong (Bolter, 1991), an issue that was also surveyed by a remarkable collection of writings edited by Thomas Farrell and Paul Soukup (2012). Lewis Mumford's work, particularly his urban and visual survey, was studied by William Mitchell (1995, 2008), while Thomas Hughes (1983, 2004) explored his work on technology. Susan Langer's work was studied and revitalized by Donald Dryden (1997, 2003), Christine Nystrom (2006), John Powers (2006) and Robert Innis (2009).

Several educational works reveal more than one affinity with media ecology's approach. These include Kennet Gergen's *The Saturated Self* (1991), from a perspective of social psychology, and Sherry Turke's trilogy *The Second Self* (1984), *Life on the Screen* (1995), and *Alone Together* (2011), from a perspective of individual and collective psychology. The concept of *Convergence culture* proposed by Henry Jenkins (2006) calls for a systemic approach to media studies incorporated in the concept of transmedia. Other works, such as Howard Rheingold's *Smart Mobs* (2002) that revives and develops the biological metaphor introduced by media ecology, focus specifically on the Social Networks phenomenon. With *Out of Control* (1994) and *What Technology Wants* (2010), Kevin Kelly reviews some of Mumford's suggestions about the relationship between humans and technology. Nicholas Carr's *The Shallows: What the Internet Is Doing to Our Brains* (2010), on the other hand, revives a host of insights proposed by McLuhan, Havelock, and Ong in order to observe the current media environment's impact our psyche and senses. A wide range of brilliant insights about the media's enveloping and environmental nature emerge from

Douglas Rushkoff's works *Program or be Programmed* (2011) and *Present Shock: When Everything Happens Now* (2013). Recently, in *The Marvelous Clouds* (2015), John Durham Peters defines media as elements that compose the human world, as infrastructures combining nature and culture. The book clearly claims an environmental approach to media studies.

In Canada, many scholars are currently working on and developing McLuhan's intellectual heritage. Recently, Eric McLuhan published two works—*Theories of Communication* (2011) and *Media and Formal Cause* (2011)—that were greeted with a great critical interest. In *The Alphabet Effect* (2004), Bob Logan explored the relationship between orality and writing in the digital world, while his *McLuhan Misunderstood* (2013) reviews McLuhan's thought in a new perspective. Derrick de Kerckhove's extensive work on communication technologies and their impact on a cognitive and sensorial level can be found in *La civilisation video-chrétienne* (1990), *Brainframes* (1991), and *The Skin of Culture* (1995). David Olson proposed an ecological approach to the pedagogy of media with *Cognitive development* (1970) and a study on *Literacy and Orality* (1991). With *Printing and Hypermedia* (1997), Ronald Deibert approached the relationship among culture, politics and society viewed from a systemic perspective. Finally, Barry Wellman's *Networked* (Rainie and Wellman, 2012) is a relevant work about the society of information.

The European intellectual context offers many authors who, while not explicitly adhering to the intellectual tradition of media ecology, have provided a host of interpretive perspectives that actually concur with its premises. These include Régis Debray, who presented the concepts of *infosphère* (in *Manifestes médialogiques* (1994)) and ecology of images (*Life and Death of Image* (1992)) that are clearly in line with the tradition of media ecology. The idea of a kind of holistic, systemic, and organic conscience in the interpretation of the phenomena of human knowledge is the core of the Fritjof Capra's works: *The Tao of Physics* (1975), *The Turning Point* (1982), *The Web of Life* (1996), and *The Hidden Connections* (2002). A similar approach was adopted by Joël De Rosnay in *The Symbiotic Man* (1995).

In *The Theory of Communicative Action* (1981) Jürgen Habermas sees communication as a systemic process that effectively has a social impact based on an inclusive, and in many ways ecological, model (Grosswiler, 2001). In *Mapping World Communication* (1992) and *The Invention of Communication* (1996), Armand Mattelart provided an environmental, procedural, systemic view of communication framed in an historical perspective, in some ways anticipated by Philippe Breton in *L'utopie de la communication* (1992) and revived by Dominique Wolton in *Internet at après?* (2000). In *Toward an Ecology of Materials*, Tim Ingold (2001) adopts an ecological approach to the study of human culture that is not unlike that proposed by Matt Ridley in *Nature via Nurture* (2003). Serge Latouche revived and developed Jacques Ellul's work in *La Mégamachine* (1995) and *Jacques Ellul contre le totalitarisme technicien* (2013). In *Moralizing Technology* (2011) Peter-Paul Verbeek has instead adopted an approach to technology that in many ways evokes Lewis Mumford's insights. The concept of "infosphere" coined by Luciano Floridi and argued in his *The Fourth Revolution* (2014) mirrors an ecological approach to the philosophy of information. In *Media Life* Mark Deuze (2012) adopted an immersive view of the media environment. Carlos Scolari's *Narrativas Transmedia* (2013) explores the idea of transmedia, viewed as a systemic relationship among the different media forms. Finally, other major European intellectuals such as Bruno Latour (Van Den Eede, 2013) and Paul Virilio (Zhang, 2013) have revealed an affinity with the environmental and systemic approach of media ecology.

Bibliography

Abbott A. (1999), *Department and Discipline. Chicago Sociology at One Undred*, University of Chicago Press, Chicago.
Alihan M. (1938), *Social Ecology. A Critical Analysis*, Columbia University Press, New York.
Altheide D. (1995), *An Ecology of Communication. Cultural Formats of Control*, Aldine de Gruyter, New York.
Anton C. (2011), *Communication Uncovered. General Semantics and Media Ecology*, Institute of General Semantics, Fort Worth, Tex.
- (2013), "Georg Simmel as Unrecognized Media Ecologist", *Explorations in Media Ecology*, 12, 3&4, pp. 171-180.
Barnes S. (2002), "Media Ecology and Symbolic Interactionism", *Proceedings of the Media Ecology Association*, vol. 3, New York.
Bateson G. (1972), *Steps to an Ecology of Mind*, Chandler Pub, San Francisco.
- (1979), *Mind and Nature: A Necessary Unit*, Dutton, New York.
- (1987), *Angels Fear: Towards an Epistemology of the Sacred*, Macmillan, New York.
Becker H.S. (1999), "The Chicago School, So-Called", *Qualitative Sociology*, 22, 2, pp. 3-12.
Benjamin W. (1915-39), *Aura e choc. Saggi sulla teoria dei media*, Einaudi, Torino, 2012.
Bennet M.J., a cura di (1998), *Principi di comunicazione interculturale*, FrancoAngeli, Milano, 2002.
Berger R. (1972), *Arte e comunicazione*, Edizioni Paoline, Ferrara, 1974.
- (1991), *Il nuovo Golem*, Raffaello Cortina, Milano, 1992.
Bernardo B., a cura di (1977), *The Concept and Dynamics of Culture*, Mouton, Paris.
Bertalanffy, L. von (1969), *Teoria generale dei sistemi*, Mondadori, Milano, 2004.
Birdwhistell R.L. (1952), *Introduction to Kinesics. An Annotation System for Analysis of Body Motion and Gesture*, University of Louisville Press, Louisville.
- (1970), *Kinesics and Context. Essays on Body Motion Communication*, University of Pennsylvania Press, Philadelphia.
Blumer H. (1969), *Interazionismo simbolico. Prospettiva e metodo*, il Mulino, Bologna, 2008.

Boas F. (1911), *L'uomo primitivo*, Laterza, Roma-Bari, 1995.
Bolter J.D. (1991), *Lo spazio dello scrivere*, Vita e Pensiero, Milano, 1993.
Bolter J.D. e Grusin R. (1999), *Remediation. Competizione e integrazione tra media vecchi e nuovi*, Guerini e Associati, Milano, 2002.
Borofsky R., a cura di (1994), *L'antropologia culturale oggi*, Meltemi, Roma, 2000.
Brake T., Walker D. e Walker T. (1995), *Doing Business Internationally*, Irwin, Burr Ridge.
Braudel F. (1967), *Capitalismo e civiltà materiale. Secoli XV-XIII*, Einaudi, Torino, 1977.
Breton P. (1992), *L'utopia della comunicazione*, UTET, Torino, 1995.
Brey P. (2000), *Technology as Extension of Human Faculties*, in Mitcham C., a cura di, *Metaphysics, Epistemology, and Technology*, JAI Press, London, pp. 59-78.
Buckingham D. (2003), *Media Education. Alfabetizzazione, apprendimento e cultura contemporanea*, Centro studi Erickson, Gardolo TN, 2006.
Burgess E.W. e Bogue D.J., a cura di (1964), *Contributions to Urban Sociology*, University of Chicago Press, Chicago.
Burns T. (1992), *Erving Goffman*, Routledge, London, New York.
Capra F. (1975), *Il Tao della fisica*, Adelphi, Milano, 1982.
- (1982), *Il punto di svolta*, Feltrinelli, Milano, 1984.
- (1996), *La rete della vita*, Rizzoli, Milano, 2001.
- (2002), *La scienza della vita*, Rizzoli, Milano, 2002.
Carey J.W. (1967), "Harold Innis and Marshall McLuhan", *Antioch Review*, 27, 1, pp. 5-39.
- (1981), "McLuhan and Mumford: The Roots of Modern Media Analysis", *Journal of Communication*, 31, 3, pp.162-168.
- (1989), *Communication as Culture*, Unwin Hyman, Boston.
- (1998), "Marshall McLuhan. Geneaology and Legacy", *Canadian Journal of Communicaion*, 23, 3, pp. 293-306.
Carpenter E.S. (1970), *The Became What They Beheld*, Outerbridge & Dienstfrey, New York.
- (1992), "Remembering Explorations", *Canadian Notes & Queries*, 46, pp. 3-14.
- (2001), *That Not-So-Silent Sea*, in Theall D., *The Virtual Marshall McLuhan*, McGill-Queens University Press, Montreal, pp. 236-261.
Carr N. (2010), *Internet ci rende stupidi? Come la rete sta cambiando il nostro cervello*, Raffaello Cortina, Milano, 2011.
Cassirer E. (1923-29), *Filosofia delle forme simboliche*, Sansoni, Firenze, 1967.
- (1930), *Forma e tecnica*, in Matteucci G., a cura di, *Ernst Cassirer. Tre studi sulla "forma formans"*, Clueb, Bologna, 2003.
- (1944), *Saggio sull'uomo. Introduzione ad una filosofia della cultura*, Armando, Roma, 2000.
Castells M. (1974), *La questione urbana*, Marsilio, Venezia, 1974.

Cavell R. (2002), *McLuhan in Space. A Cultural Geography*, Univ. of Toronto Press, Toronto.
Charon J.M. (1979), *Symbolic Interactionism*, Prentice-Hall, Englewood Cliffs NJ.
Chatterjee K.R. (2002), *Understanding I.A. Rishards. Principles of Literary Criticism*, Atlantic, New Delhi.
Christian W. (1980), *The Idea Files of Harold Adams Innis*, University of Toronto Press, Toronto.
Christians C.G. e Real M.R. (1979), "Jacques Ellul's Contributions to Critical Media Theory", *Journal of Communication*, 29, 1, pp. 83-93.
Cohen M.J. (1982), *Charles Horton Cooley and the Social Self in American Thought*, Garland, New York.
Cooley C.H. (1897), *The Process of Social Change*, Ginn & Company, Boston.
– (1902), *Human Nature and the Social Order*, Scribner's Sons, New York.
– (1909), *Il gruppo primario. I processi comunicativi*, Kurumuny, Calimera LE.
Creighton D.G. (1957), *Harold Adams Innis. Portrait of a Scholar*, University of Toronto Press, Toronto.
Cuche D. (2004), *La nozione di cultura nelle scienze sociali*, il Mulino, Bologna, 2006.
Curtis J.M. (1978), *Culture as Poliphony*, University of Mussouri Press, Columbia.
Czitrom D.J. (1982), *Media and the American Mind. From Morse to McLuhan*, University of North Carolina Press, Chapel Hill.
De Kerckhove D. (1989), "Marshall McLuhan and The Toronto School of Communication", *Journal of Communication*, pp. 73-79.
– (1990), *La civilizzazione video-cristiana*, Feltrinelli, Milano, 1995.
– (1991), *Brainframes. Mente, tecnologia, mercato*, Baskerville, Bologna, 1991.
– (1995), *La pelle della cultura*, Costa & Nolan, Milano, 1996.
De Rosnay J. (1995), *L'uomo, Gaia e il Cibionte. Viaggio nel terzo millennio*, Dedalo, Bari, 1997.
Dear M., a cura di (2002), *From Chicago to L.A. Making Sense of Urban Theory*, Sage, London.
Debray R. (1992), *Vita e morte dell'immagine*, il Castoro, Milano, 1999.
– (1994), *Manifestes médialogiques*, Gallimard, Paris.
Deibert R.J. (1997), *Parchment, Printing, and Hypermedia*, Columbia Univ. Press, New York.
Demartis L. (2004), *L'estetica simbolica di Susanne Katherina Langer*, Centro Internazionale Studi di Estetica, Palermo.
Dennis E.E. e Wartella E., a cura di (1996), *American Communication Research. The Remembered History*, Erlbaum, Mahwahm NJ.
Deuze M. (2012), *Media Life*, Polity Press, Cambridge UK.
Dewey J. (1916), *Democrazia e educazione*, Sansoni, Firenze, 2004.
Diggins J.P. (1999), *Thorstein Veblen. Theorist of the Leisure Class*, Princeton University Press, Princeton.

Drache D., a cura di (1995), *Staples, Markets, and Cultural change. Selected essays by Harold Innis*, McGill-Queen's University Press, Montréal.
Dryden D. (1997), "Whitehead's Influence on Susanne Langer's Conception of Living Form", *Process-Studies*, 26, 1-2, pp. 62-85.
- (2003), *Susanne K. Langer*, in Dematteis P.B. e McHenry L.B., a cura di, *Dictionary of Literary Biography. American Philosophers before 1950*, Gale, Farmington, pp. 189-199.
Durkheim É. (1895), *Le regole del metodo sociologico*, Edizioni di Comunità, Milano, 1989.
Eco U. (1968a), *La struttura assente. Introduzione alla ricerca semiologica*, Bompiani, Milano.
- (1968b), *Edward T. Hall e la prossemica*, in Hall E.T., *La dimensione nascosta*, Bompiani, Milano, pp. V-XI.
Edmond M. e Picard D. (2006), *L'École de Palo Alto*, Retz, Paris.
Einstein A. (1956), *Pensieri, idee, opinioni*, Newton Compton, Roma, 2004.
Eisenstein E.L. (1979), *La rivoluzione inavvertita. La stampa come fattore di mutamento*, il Mulino, Bologna, 1986.
Ekman P. (1985), *I volti della menzogna*, Giunti, 1989.
Elder B.R. (2012), *Dada, Surrealism, and the Cinematic Effect*, Wilfrid Laurier, Waterloo.
Ellul J. (1954), *La tecnica, rischio del secolo*, Giuffrè, Milano, 1969.
- (1955), *Storia delle istituzioni*, 5 voll., Mursia, Milano, 1976.
- (1962), *Propagandes*, Armand Collin, Paris.
- (1977), *Il sistema tecnico. La gabbia delle società contemporanee*, Jaca Book, Milano, 2009.
- (1987), *Ce que je crois*, Grasset, Paris.
- (1988), *Le Bluff technologique*, Hachette, Paris.
Farrel T.J. (2000), *Walter Ong's Contributions to Cultural Studies. The Phenomenology of the Word and I-thou Communication*, Hampton Press, Cresskill, NJ.
Farrel T.J. e Soukup P.A., a cura di (2012), *Of Ong and Media Ecology: Essays in Communication, Composition, and Literary Studies*, Hampton Press, New York.
Fine G.A., a cura di (1995), *A Second Chicago School? The Development of a Post war American Sociology*, University of Chicago Press, Chicago.
Flayhan D. (2002), "Hidden Dimensions of Hall in Media Ecology", *Proceedings of the Media Ecology Association*, vol. 3, pp. 1-20.
Flichy P. (1995), *L'innovazione tecnologica*, Feltrinelli, Milano, 1996.
Floridi L. (2009), *Infosfera. Etica e filosofia nell'età dell'informazione*, Giappichelli, Torino.
- (2010), *La rivoluzione dell'informazione*, Codice Edizioni, Torino, 2012.
- (2014), *The Fourth Revolution*, Oxford University Press, Oxford.
Flusser V. (1983), *Per una filosofia della fotografia*, Bruno Mondadori, Milano, 2006.
- (1985), *Immagini*, Fazi editore, Roma, 2009.

- (1992), *La cultura dei media*, Bruno Mondadori, Milano, 2004.
Foucault M. (1975), *Sorvegliare e punire. Nascita della prigione*, Einaudi, Torino, 2005.
Forsdale L. (1981), *Perspectives on communication*, Random House, New York.
- (1989), *Marshall McLuhan e le regole del gioco*, in Sanderson G. e MacDonald F., a cura di, *Marshall McLuhan. L'uomo e il suo messaggio,* SugarCo, Milano, 1994, pp. 171-181.
Fraser P. e Wardle J., a cura di (2013), *Current Perspectives in Media Education: Beyond the Manifesto*, Palgrave Macmillan, Houndmills UK.
Fuller R.B. (1938), *Nine Chains to the Moon*, Lippincott, New York.
Gadamer H-G. (1960), *Verità e metodo*, Bompiani, Milano, 2000.
Gannaway G. (1994), *Transforming Mind. A Critical Cognitive Activity*, Bergin & Garvey, Westport.
Gardner H. (1982), *Art, Mind, and Brain*, Basic Books, New York.
Geddes P. (1915), *Città in evoluzione*, il Saggiatore, Milano, 1984.
Gehlen A. (1940), *L'uomo. La sua natura e il suo posto nel mondo*, Feltrinelli, Milano, 1983.
Gencarelli T.F. (2000), "The Intellectual Roots of Media Ecology in the Thought and Work of Neil Postman", *The New Jersey Journal of Communication*, 8, 1, pp. 91-103.
- (2006), *Neil Postman and the Rise of Media Ecology*, in Lum C.M.K., a cura di, *Perspectives on Culture, Technology and Communication*, Hampton Press, Cresskill, NJ, pp. 201-253.
Georgiadis S. (1993), *Sigfried Giedion. An Intellectual Biography*, Edinburgh University Press, Edinburgo.
Gergen K.J. (1991), *The Saturated Self*, Basic Books, New York.
Gilloch G. (2002), *Walter Benjamin*, il Mulino, Bologna, 2008.
Goffman E. (1959), *La vita quotidiana come rappresentazione*, il Mulino, Bologna, 1969.
- (1967), *Il rituale dell'interazione*, il Mulino, Bologna, 1988.
- (1974), *Frame Analysis. L'organizzazione dell'esperienza*, Armando, Roma, 1998.
Goody J. (1977), *L'addomesticamento del pensiero selvaggio*, FrancoAngeli, Milano, 1981.
- (1987), *Il suono e i segni. L'interfaccia tra scrittura e oralità*, il Saggiatore, Milano, 1989.
- (2000), *Il potere della tradizione scritta*, Bollati Boringhieri, Torino, 2002.
Goody J. e Watt I. (1963), *Le conseguenze dell'alfabetizzazione*, in Giglioli P.P., a cura di, *Linguaggio e società*, il Mulino, Bologna, 1973, pp. 361-405.
Gordon W.T. (1997), *Marshall McLuhan. Escape into Understanding*, BasicBooks, New York.
Gozzi R. (2000), "Jacques Ellul on Technique, Media, and the Spirit", *New Jersey Journal of Communication*, 8, 1, pp. 79-90.
Greenman J.P., Schuchardt R.M. e Toly N.J. (2013), *Understanding Jacques*

Ellul, James Clarke & co. Cambridge, UK.
Griffin E. (2012), *A First Look at Communication Theory*, McGraw-Hill, New York.
Gronbeck B.E. (2006), *The Orality-Literacy Theorems and Media Ecology*, in Lum C.M.K., a cura di, *Perspectives on Culture, Technology and Communication: The Media Ecology Tradition*, Hampton Press, Cresskill, NJ, pp. 335-265.
Gronbeck B.E., Farrel T.J. e Soukup P.A., a cura di (1991), *Media, Consciousness and Culture. Explorations of Walter Ong's Thought*, Sage, Thousand Oaks, CA.
Grosswiler P. (1998), *The Method is the Message. Rethinking McLuhan Through Critical Theory*, Black Rose Books, Montréal.
– (2001), "Jürgen Habermas: Media Ecologist?", *Proceedings of the Media Ecology Association*, 2, pp. 22-31.
Guardiani F. (1991), "Il postmoderno esce dal caos. Verso la sintesi di McLuhan e Frye", *Adl*, p, pp. 56-71.
– (1996), "The Common Ground of McLuhan and Frye", *McLuhan Studies*, 1, pp. 1-14.
Guichard É. (2012), *Ecritures. Sur les traces de Jack Goody*, Presses de l'enssib, Villeurbanne.
Gumpert G. (1988), *Talking Tombstones and Other Tales of the Media Age*, Oxford University Press, New York.
Habermas J. (1981), *Teoria dell'agire comunicativo*, il Mulino, Bologna, 1986.
Hall E.T. (1959), *Il linguaggio silenzioso*, Bompiani, Milano, 1969.
– (1966), *La dimensione nascosta*, Bompiani, Milano, 1968.
– (1976), *Beyond Culture*, Doubleday, Garden City, NY.
– (1983), *The Dance of Life. The Other Dimension of Time*, Doubleday, Garden City, NY.
– (1992), *An Anthropology of Everyday Life. An Autobiography*, Doubleday, New York.
Halton E. (1995), *Bereft of Reason. On the Decline of Social Thought and Prospects for its Renewal*, University of Chicago Press, Chicago.
Hannerz U. (1980), *Esplorare la città. Antropologia della vita urbana*, il Mulino, Bologna, 1992.
Hardt H. (1992), *Critical Communication Studies. Communication, History, and Theory in America*, Routledge, London-New York.
Harms W. E DePencier I., a cura di (1996), *Experiencng Education. 100 Years of Learning at The University of Chicago Laboratory Schools*, The University of Chicago Laboratory Schools, Chicago.
Harries-Jones P. (2009), *Come l'epistemologia di Bateson ha cambiato la cibernetica di Wiener*, in Bertrando P. e Bianciardi M., a cura di, *La natura sistemica dell'uomo. Attualità del pensiero di Gregory Bateson*, Raffaello Cortina, Milano, pp. 69-84.
Harris M. (1968), *L'evoluzione del pensiero antropologico*, il Mulino, Bologna, 1971.

- (1979), *Materialismo culturale*, Feltrinelli, Milano, 1984.
Hart C., a cura di (2010), *Legacy of the Chicago School*, Midrash, Cheshire, England.
Harvey L. (1986), "The Myths of the Chicago School", *Quality and Quantity*, 20, 2-3, pp. 191-217.
Havelock E.A. (1963), *Cultura orale e civiltà della scrittura*, Laterza, Roma-Bari, 1973.
- (1976), *Dalla A alla Z. Le origini della civiltà della scrittura in Occidente*, Il Melagolo, Genova, 1987.
- (1982), *Harold Innis: a Memoir*, Harold Innis Foudation, Toronto.
- (1986a), *La Musa impara a scrivere*, Laterza, Roma-Bari, 1995.
- (1986b), "The Alphabetic Mind", *Oral Tradition*, 1, 1, pp. 134-150.
Hawley A. (1950), *Human Ecology. A Theory of Community Structure*, Ronald Press, New York.
- (1971), *Urban Society. An Ecological Approach*, Ronald Press, New York.
- (1989), *Human Ecology. A Theoretical Essay*, University of Chicago Press, Chicago.
Heims S. J. (1980), *John Von Neumann and Norbert Wiener*, MIT Press, Cambridge, MA.
Heyer P. (2003), *Harold Innis*, Rowman & Littlefield, Boulder.
- (2006), *Harold Innis' Legacy in the Media Ecology Tradition*, in Lum C.M.K., a cura di, *Perspectives on Culture, Technology and Communication: The Media Ecology Tradition*, Hampton Press, Cresskill, NJ, pp. 143-161.
Hinkle R.C. (1980), *Founding Theory of American Sociology, 1881-1915*, Routledge & Kegan Paul, Boston.
Hughes T.P e Hughes A.C., a cura di (1990), *Lewis Mumford: Public Intellectual*, Oxford University Press, New York.
Hughes T.P. (1983), *Networks of Power. The Electrification of Western Societies. 1880-1930*, Johns Hopkins University Press, Baltimore.
- (2004), *Il mondo a misura d'uomo*, Codice Edizioni, Torino, 2006.
Humboldt W. von (1820), *La diversità delle lingue*, Laterza, Roma-Bari, 2005.
Hutchison R. (2010), *Chicago School of Urban Sociology* in Hutchison R., a cura di, *Encyclopedia of Urban Studies*, Sage, London-New York, pp. 127-131.
Ingold T. (2001), *Ecologia della cultura*, Meltemi, Roma.
Innis H.A. (1950), *Impero e comunicazioni*, Meltemi, Roma, 2001.
- (1951), *Le tendenze della comunicazione*, SugarCo, Milano, 1982.
- (1952), *Changing Concepts of Time*, University of Toronto Press, Toronto.
Innis, R.E. (2009), *Susanne Langer in Focus*, Indiana University Press, Bloomington.
Jandy E.C. (1942), *Charles Horton Cooley. His Life and His Social Theory*, The Dryden Press, New York.

Jenkins H. (2006), *Cultura convergente*, Apogeo, Milano, 2007.
Jennings M.W., Doherty B. e Lebin T.Y., (2008), *Editors' Introduction*, in Benjamin W., *The Work of Art in the Age of Technological Reproduction and Other Writings on Media*, Harvard University Press, Cambridge MA.
Kaplan D. e Manners R.A. (1972), *Culture Theory*, Prentice Hall, Englewood Cliffs, NJ.
Kapp E. (1877), *Grundlinien einer Philosophie der Technik*, Neudruck, Düsseldorf, ed. 1978.
Katan D. (1999), *Translating Cultures*, Routledge, New York.
Kelly K. (1994), *Out of Control*, Urrà, Milano, 1996.
- (2010), *Quello che vuole la tecnologia*, Codice Edizioni, Torino, 2011.
Kittler F. (1985), *Discourse Networks. 1800/1900*, Stanford University Press, Stanford, 1985.
- (1986), *Gramophone, Film, Typewriter*, Stanford University Press, Stanford, 1999.
- (1996), "The City Is a Medium", *New Literary History*, 27, 4, pp. 717-729.
- (2009), "Towards an Ontology of Media", *Theory, Culture & Society*, 26, 2-3, pp. 26-31.
Kluver R. (2006), *Jacques Ellul: Technique, Propaganda, and Modern Media*, in Lum C.M.K., a cura di, *Perspectives on Culture, Technology and Communication: The Media Ecology Tradition*, Hampton Press, Cresskill, NJ, pp. 97-116.
Kroeber A.L. (1952), *La natura della cultura*, il Mulino, Bologna, 1974.
Kroeber A.L. e Kluckhohn C. (1952), *Il concetto di cultura*, il Mulino, Bologna, 1972.
Kroker A. (1984), *Technology and the Canadian Mind*, New World Perspectives, Montréal.
Kuhns W. (1971), *The Post-Industrial Prophets. Interpretations of Technology*, Weybright and Talley, New York.
Kurtz L.R. (1984), *Evaluating Chicago Sociology. A Guide to the Literature with an Annotated Bibliography*, University of Chicago Press, Chicago.
Lamberti E. (2000), *Marshall McLuhan. Tra letteratura, arte e media*, Bruno Mondadori, Milano.
- (2005), *'Integral Awareness'. Marshall McLuhan as a Man of Letters*, in Strate L. e Wachtel E., a cura di, *The Legacy of McLuhan*, Hampton Press, Cresskill, NJ.
- (2012), *Marshall McLuhan's Mosaic: Probing the Literary Origins of Media Studies*, University of Toronto Press, Toronto.
Langer S.K. (1930), *A Logical Analysis of Meaning*, Henry Holt & co., New York.
- (1937), *An Introduction to Symbolic Logic*, 1953³, Dover, New York.
- (1942), *Filosofia in una nuova chiave. Linguaggio, mito, rito e arte*, Armando, 1972.
- (1953), *Sentimento e forma. Una teoria dell'arte*, Feltrinelli, Milano, 1965.

- (1957), *Problemi dell'arte. Dieci conferenze filosofiche*, Aesthetica, Palermo, 2013.
- (1962), *Philosophical Sketches*, Johns Hopkins University Press, Baltimore.
- (1967-82), *Mind. An Essay on Human Feeling*, Johns Hopkins University Press, Baltimore.

Latouche S. (2013), *Jacques Ellul. Contro il totalitarismo tecnico*, Jaca Book, Milano, 2014.

Latouche S., a cura di (1995), *La Megamacchina. Ragione tecnoscientifica, ragione economica e mito del progresso. Saggi in memoria di Jacques Ellul*, Bollati Boringhieri.

Leavis F.R. e Thompson D. (1933), *Culture and Environment. The Training of Critical Awareness*, Chatto & Windus, London.

Leeds-Hurwitz W. (1990), "Notes in the History of Intercultural Communication", *Quarterly Journal of Speech*, 76, 3, pp. 262-281.

Leroi-Gourhan A. (1943), *L'uomo e la materia*, Jaca Book, Milano, 1993.
- (1964), *Il gesto e la parola*, Einaudi, Torino, 1977.

Levinson P. (1997), *The Soft Age*, Routledge, London & New York.
- (1999), *Digital McLuhan. A Guide to the Information Millennium*, Routledge, New York.
- (2000), "McLuhan and Media Ecology", *Proceedings of the Media Ecology Association*, vol. 1, New York, pp. 17-21.

Li S. (2009), *Lewis Mumford. Critic of Culture and Civilization*, Peter Lang, Bern.

Lipset D. (1980), *Gregory Bateson. The Legacy of a Scientist*, Beacon Press, Boston.
- (2009), *Autore ed eroe. Una rilettura della prima parte di "Bateson, l'eredità di uno scienziato"*, in Bertrando P. e Bianciardi M., a cura di, *La natura sistemica dell'uomo. Attualità del pensiero di Gregory Bateson*, Raffaello Cortina, Milano, pp. 53-68.

Logan R.K. (2004), *The Alphabet Effect. A Media Ecology Understanding of the Making of Western Civilization*, Hampton Press, Cresskill NJ.
- (2010), "The Biological Foundation of Media Ecology", *Explorations in Media Ecology*, 9, 3, pp. 141-156.
- (2013), *McLuhan Misunderstood*, Key Publishing House, Toronto.

Lucarelli M. (1995), *Lewis Mumford and the Ecological Region*, Gufolford, New York.

Luhmann N. (1984), *Sistemi sociali*, il Mulino, Bologna, 1990.
- (1986), *Comunicazione ecologica*, FrancoAngeli, Milano, 1992.
- (1996), *La realtà dei mass media*, FrancoAngeli, Milano, 2000.

Luhmann N. e De Giorgi R., (1991), *Teoria delle società*, FrancoAngeli, Milano.

Lum C.M.K., a cura di (2006), *Perspectives on Culture, Technology and Communication: The Media Ecology Tradition*, Hampton Press, Cresskill, NJ.

Lyons J. (1981), *Lezioni di linguistica*, Laterza, Roma-Bari, 1982.
Malinowski B., *Argonauti del Pacifico occidentale*, Bollati Boringhieri, Torino, 2004.
Marchand P. (1989), *Marshall McLuhan. The Medium and the Messenger*, Random House, Toronto.
Masani P.R. (1980), *Norbert Wiener: His Life and Work*, Dekker, New York.
Massie K. (2014), *Communication Connections*, Kendall Hunt, Dubuque, IA.
Mattelart A. (1992), *La comunicazione-mondo*, il Saggiatore, Milano, 2006.
– (1994), *L'invenzione della comunicazione*, il Saggiatore, Milano, 1998.
Marvin C. (1988), *When Old Technologies Were New*, Oxford Unversity Press, New York.
McKenzie R.D. (1968), *On Human Ecology*, University of Chicago Press, Chicago.
McLuhan E. (2011), *Theories of Communication*, Peter Lang, New York.
McLuhan M. (1943), *The Classical Trivium: The Place of Thomas Nashe in the Learning of His Time*, Gingko Press, Corte Madera, CA, 2006.
– (1951), *La sposa meccanica. Il folklore dell'uomo industriale*, SugarCo, Milano, 1984.
– (1959a), "Myth and Mass Media", *Daedalus*, 88, 2, pp. 339-348.
– (1959b), *Communication Media: Makers of the Modern World*, in McLuhan E. e Szklarek J., a cura di, *The Medium and the Light. Reflections on Religion*, Stoddart, Toronto, New York, pp. 33-44.
– (1960), *Report on Project in Understanding New Media*, National Association of Educational Broadcasters, U.S. Dept. of Health, Education and Welfare.
– (1961), "Inside the Five Sense Sensorium", *Canadian Architet*, 6, 6, pp. 49-54.
– (1962), *La Galassia Gutenberg. Nascita dell'uomo tipografico*, Armando, Roma, 1976.
– (1964a), *Capire i media. Gli strumenti del comunicare*, il Saggiatore, Milano, 2011.
– (1964b), *Introduzione*, in Innis H.A., *Le tendenze della comunicazione*, SugarCo, Milano, 1982, pp. 13-22.
– (1967a), "The Invisible Environment: The Future of an Erosion", *Perspecta*, 11, pp. 163-167.
– (1967b), *It Is Natural that One Medium Should Appropriate and Exploit Another?*, in Stearn G.E., a cura di, *McLuhan. Hot & Cool*, Signet Books, New York, pp. 151-160.
– (1969a), *Il Paesaggio interiore. La critica letteraria di Marshall McLuhan*, SugarCo, Milano, 1983.
– (1969b), *Intervista a Playboy. Un dialogo diretto con il gran sacerdote della cultura pop e il metafisico dei media*, FrancoAngeli, Milano, 2013.
– (1969c), *Conterblast*, McClelland and Stewart, Toronto.
– (1970), *La cultura come business*, Armando, Roma, 1998.

- (1975), "McLuhan's Laws of the Media", *Technology and Culture*, 16, 1, pp. 74-78.
- (1999), *The Medium and the Light: Reflections on Religion*, a cura di E. McLuhan e J. Szklarek, Stoddart, Toronto.

McLuhan M. e Carpenter E.S., a cura di (1960), *La comunicazione di massa*, La Nuova Italia, Firenze, 1966.

McLuhan M. e Fiore Q. (1967), *Il medium è il massaggio*, Corraini, Mantova, 2011.

- (1968), *Guerra e pace nel villaggio globale*, Apogeo, Milano, 1995.

McLuhan M. e McLuhan E. (1988), *La legge dei media: la nuova scienza*, Lavoro, Roma 1994.

- (2011), *Media and Formal Cause*, NeoPoieis, New York.

McLuhan M., McLuhan E. e Hutchon K. (1977), *La città come aula*, Armando, Roma, 1980.

McLuhan M. e Nevitt B., (1972), *Take Today. The Executive as Dropout*, Harcourt Brace Jovanovich, New York.

McLuhan M. e Parker H. (1968), *Il punto di fuga*, SugarCo, Milano, 1988.

McLuhan M. e Powers B.R. (1989), *Il villaggio globale*, SugarCo, Milano, 1998.

McLuhan M. e Watson W. (1970), *Dal cliché all'archetipo*, SugarCo, Milano, 1987.

Mead G.H. (1930), "Cooley's Contribution to American Social Thought", *American Journal of Sociology*, XXXV, 5, pp. 693-706.

- (1934), *Mente, sé e società*, Giunti, Firenze, 2010.

Meller H.E. (1990), *Patrick Geddes. Social Evolutionist and City Planner*, Routledge, London.

Melody W.H., Salter L., Heyer P., a cura di (1981), *Culture, Communication and Dependency. The Tradition of H.A. Innis*, Ablex, Norwood.

Meltzer B.N., Peras J.W. e Reynolds L.T., a cura di (2014), *Symbolic Interactionism. Genesis, Varieties and Criticism*, Routledge, London.

Meyrowitz J. (1985), *Oltre il senso del luogo*, Baskerville, Bologna, 1995.

- (2003), *Canonic Anti-Text. Marshall McLuhan's Understanding Media*, in Katz E., Peters J.D., Liebes T. e Orloff A., a cura di, *Canonic Texts in Media Research*, Polity, Cambridge.

Miller D.L. (1989), *Lewis Mumford: A Life*, Weidenfeld & Nicolson, New York.

Mitchell W.J.T. (1995), *La città dei bits*, Milano, Electa, 1997.

- (2008), *Pictorial Turn. Saggi di cultura visuale*, Duepunti, Palermo.

Molinaro M., McLuhan C. e Toye W., a cura di (1987), *Letters of Marshall McLuhan*, Oxford University Press, Toronto-New York.

Moore J.D. (2012), *Visions of Culture. An Introduction to Anthropological Theories and Theorists*, Altamira Press, Lanham, Maryland.

Morrison J.C. (2000), "Hypermedia and Synesthesia", *Proceedings of the Media Ecology Association*, vol. 1, New York, pp. 37-51.

- (2006), *Marshall McLuhan. The Modern Janus*, in Lum C.M.K., a cura

di, *Perspectives on Culture, Technology and Communication,* Hampton Press, Cresskill, NJ, pp. 163-200.
Mumford L. (1922), *Storia dell'utopia,* Calderini, Bologna, 1969.
- (1934), *Tecnica e cultura. Storia della macchina e dei suoi effetti sull'uomo,* Net, Milano, 2005.
- (1938), *La cultura delle città,* Edizioni di Comunità, Milano, 1954.
- (1944), *La condizione dell'uomo,* Etas Kompass, Milano, 1967.
- (1951), *The Conduct of Life,* Harcourt, Brace & Co., New York.
- (1952), *Arte e tecnica,* Etas Kompass, Milano, 1966.
- (1956), *Le trasformazioni dell'uomo,* Edizioni di Comunità, Milano, 1968.
- (1961), *La città nella storia,* 3 voll., Bompiani, Milano, 1977.
- (1967), *Il mito della macchina,* il Saggiatore, Milano, 1969.
- (1970), *Il pentagono del potere,* il Saggiatore, Milano, 1973.
- (1982), *Sketches from Life: Autobiography of Lewis Mumford,* Dial Press, New York.
Murphie A. e Potts J. (2003), *Culture and Technology,* Palgrave-MacMillan, New York.
Nevitt B. (1982), *The Communication Ecology. Re-presentation vs Replica,* Butterworths, Toronto.
Novak F.G., a cura di (1995), *Lewis Mumford and Patrick Geddes. The correspondence,* Routledge, London.
Nystrom C. (1971), *Towards a Science of Media Ecology,* New York University (inedito).
- (2006), *Symbols, Thought, and "Reality". The Contributions of Benjamin Lee Whorf and Susanne K. Langer to Media Ecology,* in Lum C.M.K., a cura di, *Perspectives on Culture, Technology and Communication,* Hampton Press, Cresskill, NJ, pp. 275-301.
Olson D.R. (1979), *Linguaggi, media e processi educativi,* Loescher, Torino.
Olson D.R. e Cole M. (2006), *Technology, Literacy and the Evolution of Society. Impications of the Work of Jack Goody,* Lawrence Eribaum, Mahwah, NJ.
Olson D.R. e Torrance N. (1991), *Alfabetizzazione e oralità,* Raffaello Cortina, Milano, 1995.
Ong W.J. (1958), *Ramus. Method and the Dacay of Dialogue. From the Art of Discourse to the Art of Reason,* Harward University Press, Cambridge MA.
- (1967), *La presenza della parola,* il Mulino, Bologna, 1970.
- (1973), *Conversazione sul linguaggio,* Armando, Roma, 1993.
- (1977), *Interfacce della parola,* il Mulino, Bologna, 1989.
- (1982), *Oralità e scrittura. Le tecnologie della parola,* il Mulino, Bologna, 1986.
- (1989), *McLuhan il maestro,* in Sanderson G. e MacDonald F., a cura di, *Marshall McLuhan. L'uomo e il suo messaggio,* SugarCo, Milano, 1994, pp. 9-17.

- (2002), "Ecology and Some of Its Future", *Explorations in Media Ecology*, 1, pp. 5-11.
Paglia C. (2002), "The North American Intellectual Tradition", *Explorations in Media Ecology*, 1, 2, pp. 21-30.
Park R.E. (1915), *La città. Suggerimenti per la ricerca sul comportamento umano nell'ambiente urbano*, in Rauty R., a cura di, *Società e Metropoli. La scuola sociologica di Chicago*, Donzelli, Roma, 1990, pp. 3-19.
- (1922), *The Immigrant Press and its Control*, Greenwood Press, Westport.
- (1936), "Human Ecology", *American Journal of Sociology*, XLII, pp. 1-15.
- (1950), *Una nota autobiografica*, in Rauty R., a cura di, *Società e Metropoli. La scuola sociologica di Chicago*, Donzelli, Roma, 1990, pp. 247-250.
- (1952), *Human Communities. The City and Human Ecology*, Free Press, Glencoe.
Park R.E. e Burgess E.W. (1921), *Introduction to the Science of Sociology*, University of Chicago Press, Chicago.
Park R.E., Burgess E.W. e McKenzie R.D. (1925), *La città*, Edizioni di Comunità, Milano, 1979.
Parry M. (1971), *The making of Homeric Verse*, Parry A., a cura di, Clarendon Press, Oxford.
Patterson G. (1990), *History and Communications: Harold Innis, Marshall McLuhan, the Interpretation of History*, University of Toronto Press, Toronto.
Peace W. (2004), *Leslie A. White. Evolution and Revolution in Anthropology*, University of Nebraska Press, Lincoln.
Peirce C.S. (1931-35), *Le leggi dell'ipotesi*, Bompiani, Milano, 1984.
Person J.E. (2012), "The Medium is the Mediator. The Christian Humanism od Marshall McLuhan", *Touschstone*, 25, 1.
Pietropaolo D. e Logan R.K., a cura di (2014), *McLuhan. Social Media Between Faith and Culture*, Lega Publishing, Ottawa.
Porcar C. e Hainic C. (2011), "The Interactive Dimension of Communication. The Pragmatics of Palo Alto Group", *Journal of Communication and Culture*, 1, 2, pp. 4-19.
Porquet J-L. (2003), *Jacques Ellul, l'uomo che aveva previsto (quasi) tutto*, Jaca Book, Milano, 2008.
Postman N. (1961), *Television and the Teaching of English*, Appleton, New York.
- (1970), *The Reformed English Curriculum*, in Eurich A.C., a cura di, *High School 1980. The Shape of Future in American Secondary Education*, Pitman, New York, pp. 160-168.
- (1979), *Ecologia dei media. L'insegnamento come attività conservatrice*, Armando, Roma, 1983².
- (1982), *La scomparsa dell'infanzia*, Armando, Roma, 2005.

- (1985), *Divertirsi da morire. Il discorso pubblico nell'era dello spettacolo*, Marsilio, Venezia, 2002.
- (1992), *Technopoly. La resa della cultura alla tecnologia*, Bollati Boringhieri, Torino, 1993.
- (1995), *La fine dell'educazione. Ridefinire il valore della scuola*, Armando, Roma, 1997.
- (1999), *Come sopravvivere al futuro*, Orme, Milano, 2006.
- (2000), "The Humanism of Media Ecology", *Proceedings of the Media Ecology Association*, vol. 1, New York, pp. 10-16.

Postman N. e Weingartner C. (1966), *La linguistica. Una rivoluzione nell'insegnamento*, Armando, Roma, 1974.
- (1969), *L'insegnamento come attività sovversiva*, La Nuova Italia, Firenze, 1973.
- (1971), *The Soft Revolution*, Delacorte Press, New York.

Powe B.W. (2014), *Marshall McLuhan and Northrop Frye. Apocalypse and Alchemy*, University of Toronto Press, Toronto.
Powell J.L. (2013), *Symbolic Interactionism*, Nova Science, New York.
Powers J.H. (2006), *Susanne Langer's Philosophy of Mind. Some implications for Media Ecology*, in Lum C.M.K., a cura di, *Perspectives on Culture, Technology and Communication: The Media Ecology Tradition*, Hampton Press, Cresskill, NJ, pp. 303-334.
Rainie L. e Wellman B. (2012), *Networked*, The Mit Press, Cambridge MA.
Rheingold H. (2002), *Smart Mobs*, Raffaello Cortina, Milano, 2003.
Richards I.A. (1924), *I fondamenti della critica letteraria*, Einaudi, Torino, 1972.
Richards I.A. e Ogden C.K. (1923), *Il significato del significato. Studio dell'influsso del linguaggio sul pensiero e della scienza del simbolismo*, Garzanti, Milano, 1975.
Ridley M. (2003), *Il gene agile. La nuova alleanza fra eredità e ambiente*, Adelphi, Milano, 2005.
Riesman D. (1950), *The Lonely Crowd. A Study of the Changing American Character*, Yale University Press, New Haven.
Rogers E.M. (2000), "The Extensions of Men. The Corrispondence of Marshall McLuhan and Edward T. Hall", *Mass Communication and Society*, 3, 1, pp. 117-135.
Rogers E.M., Hart W.B. e Miike Y. (2002), "Edward T. Hall and The History of Intercultural Communication", *Keio Communication Review*, 24, pp. 3-26.
Ridley M. (2003), *Il gene agile. La nuova alleanza fra eredità e ambiente*, Adelphi, Milano, 2005.
Rushkoff D. (2011), *Programma o sarai programmato*, Postmedia, Milano, 2012.
- (2013), *Presente continuo. Quando tutto accade ora*, Codice Edizioni, Torino, 2014.

Salvini A., a cura di (2012), *The Present and the Future of Symbolic Inter-

actionism. Proceedings of the International Symposium, Pisa 2010, 2 voll., FrancoAngeli, Milano.
Sanderson G. e MacDonald F., a cura di (1989), *L'uomo e il suo messaggio. Le leggi dei media, la violenza, l'ecologia, la religione*, SugarCo, Milano, 1994.
Sapir E. (1921), *Il linguaggio. Introduzione alla linguistica*, Einaudi, Torino, 1969.
Schnapp J. e Michaels A. (2012), *The Electric Information Age Book. McLuhan, Agel, Fiore and the Experimental Paperback*, Princeton Architectural Press, New York.
Schubert H.J. (2006), "The Foundation of Pragmatic Sociology: Charles Horton Cooley and George Herbert Mead", *Journal of Classical Sociology*, 6, pp. 51-74.
Scolari C.A. (2011), "Media Ecology. Map of a Theoretical Niche", *International Journal of McLuhan Studies*, 1, pp.157-169.
– (2012), "Media Ecology. Exploring the Metaphor to Expand the Theory", *Communication Theory*, 22, pp. 204-225.
– (2013), *Narrativas Transmedia. Cuando todos los medios cuentan*, Deusto, Barcelona.
Séris J-P. (1994), *La Thechnique*, Presses Universitaires de France, Paris.
Sfez L. (1990), *Critique de la communication*, Éditions de Seuil, Paris.
Shannon C.E. e Weaver W. (1949), *La teoria matematica delle comunicazioni*, Etas Kompass, Milano, 1971.
Shelley C. (1998), "Consciousness, Symbols and Aesthetics. A Jast-so Story and its Implications in Susanne Langer's *Mind*", *Philosophical-Psychology*, 11, 1, pp. 45-66.
Shils E.A. (1970), "Tradition, Ecology, and Istitution in the History of Sociology", *Daedalus*, 99, pp. 760-825.
– (1991), *Remembering the University of Chicago*, University of Chicago Press, Chicago.
Simmel G. (1903), *La metropoli e la vita dello spirito*, Armando, Roma, 1995.
Skidelsky E. (2008), *Ernst Cassirer. The Last Philosopher of Culture*, Princeton University Press, Princeton, NJ.
Smith A.G., a cura di (1966), *Communication and Culture*, Holt, Rinehart & Wiston, New York.
Smith M.R. e Marx L. (1994), *Does Technology Drive History? The Dilemma of Technological Determinism*, MIT Press, Cambridge, Mass.
Snow C.P. (1959), *Le due culture*, Marsilio, Venezia, 2005.
Spencer H. (1860), "The Social Organism", *The Westminster Review*, LXXIII, pp. 105-108.
Stagoll B. (2009), *L'eredità di Gregory Bateson*, in Bertrando P. e Bianciardi M., a cura di, *La natura sistemica dell'uomo*, Raffaello Cortina, Milano, pp. 25-52.
Stamps J. (1995), *Unthinking Modernity: Innis, McLuhan and the Frankfurt*

School, McGill-Queen's University Press, Montréal.
Stearn G.E. (1967), *McLuhan. Hot & Cool*, Signet Books, New York.
Steward J. (1955), *Teoria del mutamento culturale*, Boringhieri, Torino, 1977.
- (1968), *Cultural Ecology*, in Sills D., a cura di, *International Encyclopedia of the Social Schiences*, vol. 4, MacMillan, New York, pp. 337-344.
Strate L. (1994), "Post(modern)man, or Neil Postman as a Postmodernist", *Etc. A Review of General Semantics*, 51, 2, pp. 159-170.
- (2003), "Neil Postman, Defender of the Word", *Etc. A Review of General Semantics*, 60, 4, pp. 341-350.
- (2004), "A Media Ecology Review", *Communication Research Trends*, 23, 2, pp. 3-48.
- (2006), *Echoes and Reflections. On Media Ecology as a Field of Study*, Hampton Press, Cresskill.
- (2007), *Il tempo, la memoria e l'ecologia dei media*, in Agazzi E. e Fortunati V., a cura di, *Memoria e saperi. Percorsi transdisciplinari*, Meltemi, Roma, pp. 379-397.
- (2008), "Studing Media as Media. Marshall McLuhan and the Media Ecology Approach", *MediaTropes*, 1, pp. 127-142.
- (2010), "Korzybski, Luhmann, and McLuhan", *Proceedings of the Media Ecology Association*, vol. 11, New York, pp. 31-42.
- (2013), "Gregory Bateson and Paul Watzlawick. From the Ecology of Mind to the Pragmatics of Media Ecology", *Explorations in Media Ecology*, 12, 3-4, pp. 199-207.
- (2014), *Amazing Ourselves to Death: Neil Postman's Brave New World Revisited*, Peter Lang, New York.
- (2017), *Media Ecology: An Approach to Understanding the Human Condition*, Peter Lang, New York.
Strate L. e Lum C.M.K. (2000), "Lewis Mumford and the Ecology of Technics", *The New Jersey Journal of Communication*, 8, 1, pp. 56-78.
Strate L. e Wachtel E., a cura di (2005), *The Legacy of McLuhan*, Hampton, Cresskill, NJ.
Subtil F.B. (2008), *James Carey and the Legacy of Chicago School of Sociology on Communication and Media Studies*, International Sociological Association, Barcelona.
Tatarkiewicz W. (1975), *Storia di sei idee*, Aesthetica, Palermo, 2011.
Theall D.F. (1986), "McLuhan, Telematics and the Toronto School of Communications", *Canadian Journal of Political and Social Theory*, 10, 1-2, pp. 79-88.
- (2001), *The Virtual Marshall McLuhan*, McGill-Queens University Press, Montreal.
Thomas J. (1983), "The Chicago School. The Tradition and the Legacy", *Urban Quarterly*, 11, 4, pp. 387-511.
Thomas W.I., Znaniecki F. (1918), *Il contadino polacco in Europa e in America*, Edizioni di Comunità, Milano, 1968.

Tilman R. (1992), *Thorstein Veblen and His Critics*, Princeton University Press, Princeton.
Troude-Chastenet P. (1992), *Lire Ellul, introduction a l'oeuvre socio-politique de Jacques Ellul*, Presses universitaires de Bordeaux, Bordeaux.
Tucker K. (2006), *Chicago School of Sociology*, in Turner B., a cura di, *The Cambridge Dictionary of Sociology*, Cambridge University Press, Cambridge.
Turkle S. (1984), *Il secondo io*, Frassinelli, Milano, 1985.
- (1995), *La vita sullo schermo*, Apogeo, Milano, 1997.
- (2011), *Insieme ma soli*, Codice Edizioni, Torino, 2012.
Tylor E.B. (1871), *Alle origini della cultura*, Edizioni dell'Ateneo, Roma, 1971.
Van Den Eede Y. (2013), "Opening the media-ecological black box of Latour", *Explorations in Media Ecology*, 12, 3-4, pp. 259-266.
Veblen T. (1899), *La teoria della classe agiata*, Einaudi, Torino, 2007.
Verbeek P-P. (2011), *Moralizing Technology*, Chicago University Press, Chicago.
Wallace D.F. (1995), *Questa è l'acqua*, Einaudi, Torino, 2009.
Wasser F. (2006), *James Carey: the Search for Cultural Balance*, in Lum C.M.K., a cura di, *Perspectives on Culture, Technology and Communication: The Media Ecology Tradition*, Hampton Press, Cresskill, NJ, pp. 255-274.
Warnier J-P. (1999), *La cultura materiale*, Meltemi, Roma, 2005.
Watson A.J. (2006), *Marginal Man. The Dark Vision of Harold Innis,* University of Toronto Press, Toronto.
Watson R. e Blondheim M., a cura di (2007), *The Toronto School of Communication Theory. Interpretations, Extensions, Applications*, University of Toronto Press, Toronto.
Watzlawick P., Beavin J.H. e Jackson D.D. (1967), *Pragmatica della comunicazione umana*, Astrolabio, Roma, 1971.
Weeks D.L. e Hoogestraat J.A., cura di (1998), *Time, Memory and the Verbal Arts: Essays on the Thought of Walter Ong*, Associated University Presses, Cranbury, NJ.
White L.A. (1949), *Scienza della cultura*, Sansoni, Firenze, 1969.
- (1959), *The Evolution of Culture*, McGraw-Hill, New York.
Whorf B.L. (1956), *Linguaggio, pensiero e realtà*, Bollati Boringhieri, Torino, 1977.
Wiener N. (1950), *Introduzione alla cibernetica*, Bollati Boringhieri, Torino, 1966.
Williams K. (2003), *Understanding Media Theory*, Arnold, London.
Willmott G. (1996), *McLuhan, or Modernism in Reverse*, University of Toronto Press, Toronto.
Winkin Y. e Leeds-Hurwitz W. (2013), *Erving Goffman*, Peter Lang, New York.
Winkin Y., a cura di (1981), *La nouvelle communication*, Éditions de Seuil, Paris.

Winthrop-Young G. (2011), *Kittler and the Media*, Polity Press, Cambridge UK.
Wirth L. (1928), *Il ghetto*, Edizioni di Comunità, Milano, 1968.
– (1945), "Human Ecology", *American Journal of Sociology*, 50, pp. 483-488.
Wolton D. (2000), *Internet... e poi? Teoria critica dei nuovi media*, Dedalo, Bari, 2001.
Zhang P. (2013), "Media Ecology and Techno-Ethic in Paul Virilio", *Explorations in Media Ecology*, 12, 3-4, pp. 241-257.
Zingrone F. (2001), *The Media Simplex*, Stoddart, Toronto.

P. Geddes

N. Frye

H. Innis   J. Tyrwhitt   J. Goody   C. Ogden
                  Toronto   F.R. Leavis   **Cambridge UK**
              E & M. McLuhan
R. Park   T. Veblen   E. Carpenter   E. Havelock   I.A. Richards
J. Dewey
C. Cooley   Chicago   E. Burgess
            R. McKenzie
      G. Mead   A. Leroi-Gourhan
                              W.J. Ong   J. Ellul   **France**
J. Carey   R. Girard   F. Braudel
    E. Goffman   E. Eisenstein   L. Forsdale
L. White   E. T. Hall   V. Flusser
                                                                           R. Berger
A. Kroeber   J. Culkin   L. Mumford   E. Cassirer
      M. Mead   F. Boas   **New York**   E. Kapp   G. Simmel
G. Bateson   N. Postman   S. Langer   **Central Europe**
    R. Birdwhistell   W. Benjamin   N. Luhmann
P. Watzlawick   A. Korzybski   N. Wiener   F. Kittler
  Palo Alto   J. Steward   L. von Bertalanffy
D. Jackson   J. Beavin   S. Giedion
            M. Harris
        D. Lee   W. James   MIT
            B. Whorf   **Harvard**
                E. Sapir   M. Parry
                    Yale

PAOLO GRANATA is an educator, an innovator, and a cross-disciplinary media scholar. Nurtured by the centuries-old tradition of his Alma Mater—the University of Bologna—his research and teaching interests lie broadly in the area of media ecology, media ethics, semiotics, print culture, and visual studies.

Over the last 20 years of his academic career in research, teaching, and public engagement, he has held positions at the University of Bologna, the Academy of Fine Arts in Bologna and Turin, and most recently at St. Michael's College in the University of Toronto, with affiliation in the Department of Italian Studies, the School of Cities, and the Schwartz Reisman Institute for Technology and Society. He has served on a variety of committees related to academic programming, curriculum review, and research development.

He authored four books—*Arte in Rete* (2001), *Arte, Estetica e Nuovi Media* (2009), *Mediabilia* (2012), and *Ecologia dei Media* (2015)—and more than 50 publications (essays, articles, book-chapters, and policy reports) in Italian, English, French, and Spanish.

From 2015 to 2017, in his capacity as Visiting Professor at the iSchool Faculty of Information, University of Toronto, he was Program Curator at the McLuhan Centre for Culture and Technology, University of Toronto. As a cultural strategist and an advocate of sustainable development, in 2017 his research and consultancy activity led to the designation of Toronto as a UNESCO Creative City of Media Arts.

Serving since 2018 as a board member of the Executive Committee at the Canadian Commission for UNESCO, his advocacy efforts are focused on digital equity and digital sustainability, exploring the potential that information and communication technologies hold for enacting positive social change.

Professor Granata is passionate about safeguarding human rights in the digital sphere. As such, in 2019, he founded the Media Ethics Lab, a research hub that studies the ways that digital media practices and emerging technologies are marked by ethical issues and decisive political, societal, and cultural questions. Since 2020, the Media Ethics Lab has been partnering with the City of Toronto on a research project to map Toronto's digital divide and to advance ConnectTO, a City-driven collaborative program that aims to increase digital equity and access to affordable internet in Toronto.

Professor Granata speaks regularly on the future of education. His aim is to raise public awareness about the role that Universities should play in the 21st century: to provide an environment of social cohesion; to create the conditions for sustainable development; and to strengthen participation in cultural life.

Made in United States
Troutdale, OR
08/18/2024